BEAD FANTASIES II

More Beautiful, Easy-to-Make Jewelry

SAMEJIMA TAKAKO

©2003 by Takako Samejima

Translated by Connie Prener

©2005 English tex., Japan Publications Trading Co., Ltd.
English edition by Japan Publications Trading Co.,Ltd.
1-2-1, Sarugaku-cho, Chiyoda-ku, Tokyo 101-0064, Japan

Original Japanese edition published by Nihon Bungei-sha Co., Ltd.,
1-7 Kanda Jinbo-cho, Chiyoda-ku, Tokyo 101-8407, Japan.

First edition, First printing : July 2005
            Second printing : August 2005

Distributors:
United States: Kodansha America, Inc. through Oxford University Press,
   198 Madison Avenue, New York, NY 10016.
Canada: Fitzhenry & White Side Ltd., 195 All States Parkway, Ontario, L3R 4T8.
Australia and New Zealand: Bookwise International Pty Ltd.
   174 Cormack Road, Wingfield, SA 5013, Australia.
Asia and other countries: Japan Publications Trading Co., Ltd.,
   1-2-1, Sarugaku-cho, Chiyoda-ku, Tokyo 101-0064, Japan.

ISBN-13: 978-4-88996-188-1
ISBN-10: 4-88996-188-7

Printed in Japan

CONTENTS

NOTES: Read These Notes And The Instructions On PP. 82-84 Before You Begin A Project.

◆If your vendor doesn't carry the designer beads or gemstones specified in this book, feel free to substitute beads of the same size and shape.

◆In our list of supplies for each project, we include approximate lengths for nylon thread and wire. Since the holes in gemstone beads are traditionally very small, we recommend using thin nylon thread.

◆Drawings: When it is not obvious where you should begin or end a particular step, we have marked our drawings as follows: the starting point is represented by a ★ symbol and the ending point with a ☽ symbol. Also, when we want you to set aside a length of nylon thread temporarily, we have written "Set aside" in our drawings.

PART 1

MOTIFS

First we created a motif. Then we used it as the centerpiece of three separate articles of jewelry. When you want the motif to be the star, make a ring or earrings. When you use a motif in a necklace or bracelet, you'll sometimes find that it is totally transformed by the beads you combine it with. Try making coordinating sets — you're sure to be delighted with the results.

CLOVER MOTIF

This delicate, three-leaf clover will put you and everyone
who sees it in a good mood.

CLOVER

Here we used teardrop peridot beads for the clover leaves. Joining the leaves with wire gives the motif a light and airy look. To make the necklaces, we added pearl or brown beads, both of which accentuate the green in the leaves. Instructions: p. 8.

PEARL NECKLACE

For this necklace, we designed a color scheme that is both bright and subtle. Pearl and gemstone beads add a note of elegance. Instructions: p. 9

EARRINGS

These lovely earrings are so simply constructed that they can be completed in a matter of minutes. Instructions: p. 8

BROWN NECKLACE

The dark brown beads form a perfect partnership with the motifs, which are arranged in a charmingly off-kilter way. Instructions: p. 9

(1) String a peridot bead on 50cm wire (A).

(2) Twist wire to secure bead (B).

(3) String another peridot bead on wire (C).

(4) Wrap wire around wire at base (narrow ends of beads) (C).

(5) String third peridot bead on wire; bring wire over to wire at base of beads.

(6) Motif should look like this after wire has been wound around base of all three beads.

(7) Wind wire twice, then set one end aside (D).

(8) Turn motif so right side is facing you; wind other end of wire once around base (E).

(9) Wind wire twice more; turn motif over to wrong side.

(10) Cut this end of wire, as well as end of wire set aside in (7).

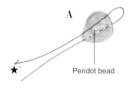

A

★

Peridot bead

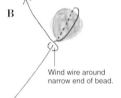

B

Wind wire around narrow end of bead.

C

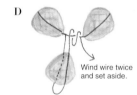

D

Wind wire twice and set aside.

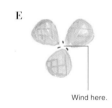

E

Wind here.

EARRINGS

Supplies

6 7-mm teardrop peridot beads, wire (2 30-cm and 2 50-cm lengths), ear wires

Instructions

(1) Make two motifs with loops, as directed in (1) and (2) of instructions for pearl necklace.
(2) Attach ear wires.

Ear wires

Make a wire loop, following instructions for pearl necklace.

PEARL NECKLACE

Supplies

3 7-mm teardrop peridot beads, 24 3.5-mm button peridot beads, 50 white 3.5-mm round freshwater pearl beads, 48 2-mm round moss agate beads, 24 4-mm button citrine beads, 2 crimp beads, spring clasp, adjustable chain closure, wire (1 30-cm length, 1 50-cm length), 60cm nylon-coated wire

Instructions

(1) Make motif; run a new length of wire through loop extending from motif; twist wire twice.

(2) Form a wire loop with round-nose pliers; twist wire and cut excess (A).

(3) Pass nylon-coated wire through motif; string beads, referring to **a** in drawing (B). Attach spring clasp to one end and adjustable chain closure to other with crimp beads.

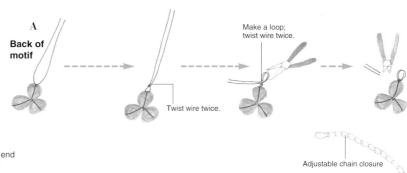

A

Back of motif

Twist wire twice.

Make a loop; twist wire twice.

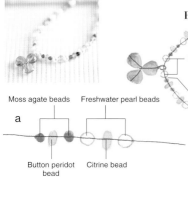

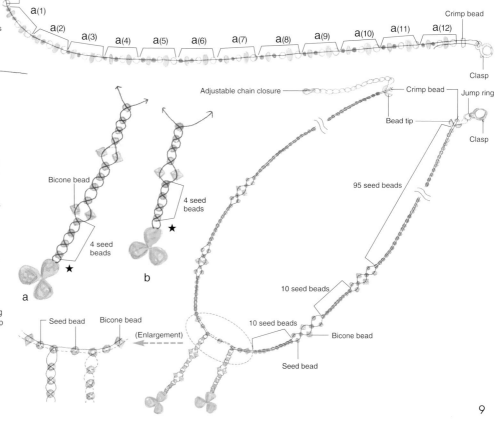

Adjustable chain closure

Crimp bead

B

Freshwater pearl bead

a(1)

a(2)

a(3) a(4) a(5) a(6) a(7) a(8) a(9) a(10) a(11) a(12)

Crimp bead

Clasp

Moss agate beads

Freshwater pearl beads

a

Button peridot bead

Citrine bead

Adjustable chain closure

Crimp bead

Jump ring

Bead tip

Clasp

95 seed beads

Bicone bead

4 seed beads

4 seed beads

a

b

★

★

10 seed beads

10 seed beads

Bicone bead

Seed bead

Seed bead   Bicone bead

(Enlargement)

BROWN NECKLACE

Supplies

6 7-mm teardrop peridot beads, 16 green 3-mm bicone crystal beads, 277 brown 2-mm seed beads, 2 bead tips, 2 crimp beads, 4-mm jump ring, spring clasp, adjustable chain closure, 2 50-cm lengths wire, 2 80-cm lengths nylon thread

Instructions

(1) Make motif; insert nylon thread into wire on back of motif; make **a** and **b**.

(2) Pass thread extending from right side of **a** through a seed bead, the seed bead at the end of **b**; pass thread extending from left side of **b** through the seed bead at the end of **a**.

(3) String beads on both threads, referring to drawing; attach a bead tip and crimp bead to each end of necklace, then clasp and adjustable chain closure.

RETRO FLOWER

This feminine design has a sophistication that appeals in any age.

BRACELET

This delicate four-strand bracelet was designed to contrast with the bold flower motif. Instructions: p. 13.

NECKLACE

The fringe on this necklace, with its shell and freshwater pearl beads, complements the motif. The chain is decorated with pearl beads on headpins, which sway as you move. Instructions: p. 13.

RING

The retro flower motif is the star in this piece. The band is fashioned from three-cut beads, which sparkle beautifully, as do the shell petals. Instructions: p. 12.

MOTIF2

RETRO FLOWER

This motif could have been designed in the 1960s, but the beads that are added to make this gorgeous necklace bring it into the 21st century. Mother-of-pearl and shell beads add a quiet luster. Instructions: p. 12.

11

(1) String a shell bead, a 3-cut bead and a seed bead on the center of 80cm nylon thread (A).

(2) Cross ends over one another with a shell bead at the intersection (A).

(3) Repeat (2) six times; close circle by crossing ends over one another with first shell bead strung at the intersection (B).

(4) Run thread through 3-cut and seed beads on front of flower (C).

(5) Repeat on back of flower (D).

(6) Bring thread out on front of flower; form an intersection in a seed bead.

(7) String mother-of-pearl bead for center (E).

(8) Pass one end of thread through a seed bead (E).

(9) Back of flower should look like this.

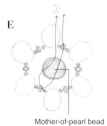

(10) Tie threads together, hide ends in beads and cut excess (E).

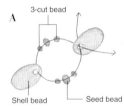

A   3-cut bead

Shell bead   Seed bead

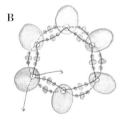

B

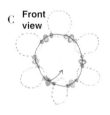

C **Front view**

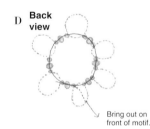

D **Back view**

Bring out on front of motif.

E

Mother-of-pearl bead

RING

Supplies

8-mm round mother-of-pearl bead, 6 brown 10-mm coin-shaped shell beads, 38 brown 3-mm seed beads, 60 bronze 1.8-mm 3-cut beads, 2 80-cm lengths nylon thread

Instructions

(1) Make motif; to make band, pick up a seed bead on back of motif using new thread, and string beads as shown in drawing.

(2) Tie threads together, hide ends in beads and cut excess.

Back view

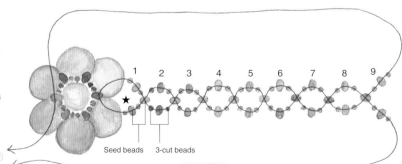

1   2   3   4   5   6   7   8   9

Seed beads   3-cut beads

BRACELET

Supplies

8-mm round mother-of-pearl bead, 6 brown 10-mm coin-shaped shell beads, 16 brown 3-mm seed beads, 384 bronze 1.8-mm 3-cut beads, 2 bead tips, 2 crimp beads, 4-mm jump ring, lobster clasp, adjustable chain closure, nylon thread (4 50-cm lengths, 1 80-cm length)

Instructions

(1) Make motif; with new thread, pick up a seed bead on back of motif; add more beads, as shown in drawing; repeat on opposite side.
(2) Attach a bead tip and crimp bead to each end, then lobster clasp and adjustable chain closure.

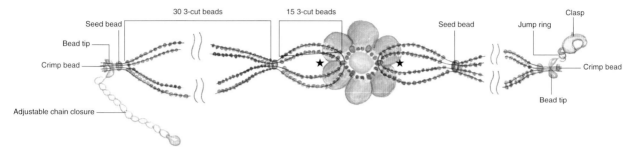

30 3-cut beads

15 3-cut beads

Seed bead

Clasp

Jump ring

Seed bead

Bead tip

Crimp bead

Crimp bead

Adjustable chain closure

Bead tip

NECKLACE

Supplies

8-mm round mother-of-pearl bead, 9 brown 10-mm coin-shaped shell beads, 12 brown 3-mm seed beads, 24 brown 1.8-mm 3-cut beads, 13 orange 3.5-mm round freshwater pearl beads, 13 thin 2-cm headpins, chain (1 each 2.5-cm, 3-cm and 4.5-cm lengths; 4 25-cm lengths), 7 4-mm jump rings, spring clasp, adjustable chain closure, 80cm nylon thread

Instructions

(1) Make motif; make Components a-c.
(2) Assemble necklace, referring to A.
(3) Attach spring clasp to one end and adjustable chain closure to other with jump rings (B).

Components

a

Chain (Make 3, one each with 2.5cm, 3cm, 4.5cm chain.)

Jump ring

Shell bead

b (Make 13.)

Headpin

Freshwater pearl bead

C (Make 4.)

25cm chain

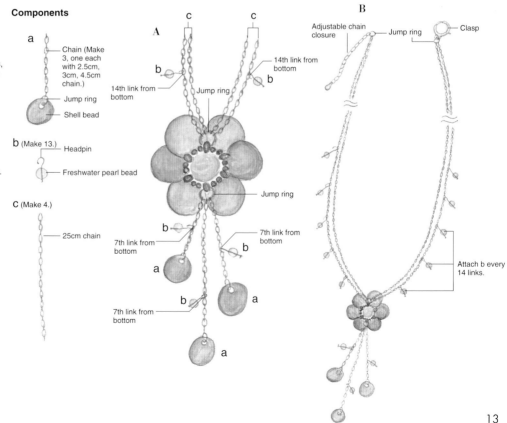

A

c

c

b

14th link from bottom

14th link from bottom

b

Jump ring

Jump ring

b

7th link from bottom

7th link from bottom

b

a

a

b

a

7th link from bottom

a

B

Adjustable chain closure

Jump ring

Clasp

Attach b every 14 links.

MOTIF3
ORIENTAL WREATH

Teardrop beads seem to float within the bead circles of these
airy, Asian-inspired motifs.

MOTIF3
ORIENTAL WREATH

Red teardrop beads on eyepins dangle from the Asian-inspired wreaths that grace earrings and two styles of necklace. To make perfect circles, use a ring stick. Instructions: p. 16

NECKLACE

This simple, sleek necklace features three motifs symmetrically placed at the center. We used one fewer button bead on each side of the two outer motifs to achieve an ideal balance. Instructions: p. 17

EARRINGS

These easy-to-make earrings are long, but since the motif has a translucent look, the total impression is one of lightness. Instructions: p. 16

NECKLACE WITH MULTIPLE MOTIFS

This dazzling necklace in a modified bib style features nine wreath motifs. Instructions: p. 17

15

(1) String 22 red seed beads on a 4-cm eyepin.

(2) Leaving a 2-3-mm space, round end with round-nose pliers (A).

(3) Form a circle, using end of ring stick (B).

(4) Remove beads from ring stick, try ring on and make fine adjustments (C).

(5) String 28 iridescent purple seed beads on a 5-cm eyepin; round end with pliers (D).

(6) Make components, using headpins and eyepins (E).

(7) String headpin components and two circles on a jump ring (F).

(8) Close jump ring with flat-nose pliers (F).

(9) Attach eyepin components to a jump ring (G).

(10) The completed earring should look like this.

A

4-cm eyepin   Leave a 2-3-mm space.

22 seed beads (red)

B

Ring stick

C

Adjust with your fingers.

D

28 seed beads (iridescent purple)

(Make 1.)

5-cm eyepin

E

Components

Headpin — 2-cm eyepin

Teardrop bead — Button bead

(Make 1.)   (Make 3.)

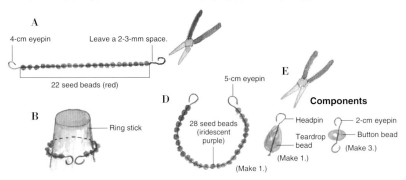

F

6-mm jump ring

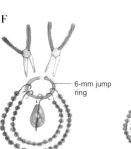

G

EARRINGS

Supplies

44 red and 56 iridescent purple 2-mm seed beads, 2 red 7 x 5-mm designer teardrop beads, 6 red 3 x 5-mm designer button beads, eyepins (6 2-cm, 2 each 4-cm and 5-cm), 2 2-cm headpins, 2 6-mm jump rings, ear wires

Instructions

(1) Make two motifs.
(2) Attach ear wires.

Ear wires

16

NECKLACE

Supplies

66 red and 84 iridescent purple 2-mm seed beads, 3 red 7 x 5-mm designer teardrop beads, 7 red 3 x 5-mm designer button beads, eyepins (7 2-cm; 3 each 4-cm and 5-cm), 3 2-cm headpins, 2 4-mm and 3 6-mm jump rings, 38cm designer chain, spring clasp, adjustable chain closure

Instructions

(1) Make motifs; attach motifs to chain as shown in drawing (shorten two of the motifs by using one fewer button bead).

(2) Attach clasp to one end of necklace and adjustable chain closure to other with jump rings.

GOLD NECKLACE

Supplies

82 gold, 198 red and 252 iridescent purple 2-mm seed beads; 86 gold 3-mm round fire-polished beads, 9 red 7 x 5-mm designer teardrop beads, 5 red 3 x 5-mm designer button beads, eyepins (9 each 2-cm, 4-cm and 5-cm), 5 2-cm headpins, 2 crimp beads, 9 6-mm jump rings, spring clasp, adjustable chain closure, 60cm nylon-coated wire

Instructions

(1) Make motif, adjusting instructions and referring to A.

(2) String motif and additional beads on nylon-coated wire, referring to B; attach clasp to one end of necklace and adjustable chain closure to other.

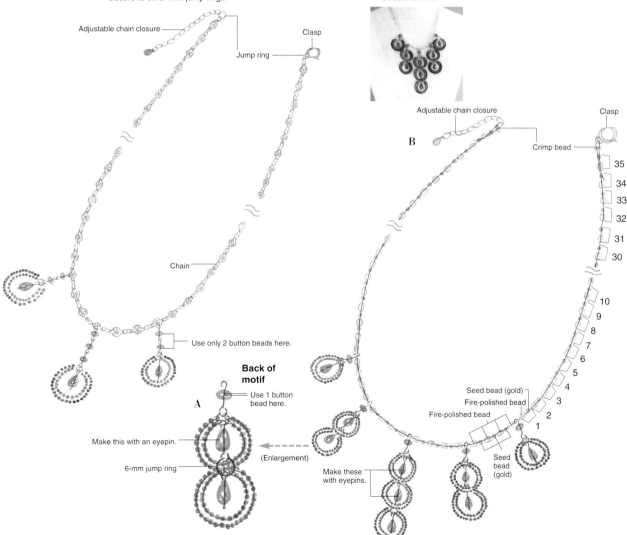

Adjustable chain closure

Clasp

Jump ring

Chain

Use only 2 button beads here.

Back of motif

Use 1 button bead here.

A

Make this with an eyepin.

6-mm jump ring

(Enlargement)

Adjustable chain closure

Clasp

Crimp bead

B

35
34
33
32
31
30

10
9
8
7
6
5
4
3
2
1

Seed bead (gold)
Fire-polished bead
Fire-polished bead

Seed bead (gold)

Make these with eyepins.

ROMANTIC FLOWER
This design suggests grace and glamour at the same time.

RING

This large (3.5cm) motif makes a beautiful ring. The side view of the design is as fascinating as the top view. Instructions: p. 21.

NECKLACE

We used amazonite beads as accents in the two-strand necklace, with spectacular results. Instructions: p. 21.

BRACELET

The bronze and pink beads on the band extend the color scheme of the motif. We placed an additional amazonite bead in the center of the motif. Instructions: p. 21.

MOTIF4

ROMANTIC FLOWER

The smoky blue of the amazonite beads contrasts beautifully with the pink of the glass beads. Bronze beads add an antique tinge. Though the feature of this piece is the twisted ropes of beads that seem impossibly intricate, this motif is not hard to make. Instructions: p. 20

19

(1) String glass beads and an amazonite bead on center of 100cm thread (A).

(2) Form an intersection in 2 glass beads (A).

(3) Repeat this pattern 7 times, then form an intersection in an amazonite bead; set one end of thread aside (B).

(4) String 18 seed beads on other end of thread, then pass thread through next amazonite bead (C).

(5) On second round, pass thread under seed beads and through amazonite beads (C).

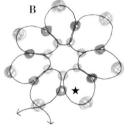

(6) Once you've worked 2 rounds, set thread aside (D).

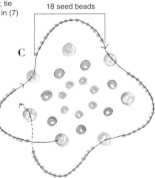

(7) String 7 glass beads on thread set aside in (3), then pass thread through an amazonite bead (E).

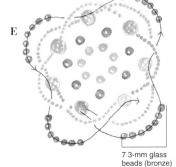

(8) Work 2 rounds in this way; tie thread to thread set aside in (7) (F).

Note: Refer to instructions for individual pieces for placement of central amazonite bead.

A

Glass bead (pink)

★

4-mm glass bead (bronze)

Amazonite bead

B

Set aside. *Tape thread not in use to work surface.

★

C

18 seed beads

D

Set aside.

E

7 3-mm glass beads (bronze)

F

BRACELET

Supplies

10 6-mm round amazonite beads, 9 bronze and 10 pink 4-mm round glass beads, 143 bronze 3-mm round glass beads, 338 pink 1-mm seed beads, 2 bead tips, 2 crimp beads, 4-mm jump ring, spring clasp, adjustable chain closure, nylon thread (2 50-cm lengths, 3 100-cm lengths)

Instructions

(1) Tape down one end of each of 2 100-cm lengths nylon thread; string beads on threads (A); pass threads through center of motif and amazonite bead.

(2) Work back to a pink glass bead, form an intersection in it; work opposite side in the same way; tape ends down (B).

(3) String seed beads on 50cm nylon thread, as shown in C; remove tape, and string a crimp bead and bead tip on thread; attach clasp and adjustable chain closure.

A

Amazonite bead

5 3-mm glass beads (bronze)

14 3-mm glass beads (bronze)

Bead tip

Tape

3-mm glass bead (bronze)

Amazonite bead

4-mm glass bead (bronze)

Glass bead (pink)

★

B Bead tip

Tape

C

Clasp

Jump ring

Crimp bead

Adjustable chain closure

Crimp bead

★

★

15 seed beads

38 seed beads

RING

Supplies

8 6-mm round amazonite beads, 7 bronze and 10 pink 4-mm round glass beads, 49 bronze 3-mm round glass beads, 38 3-mm bronze round fire-polished beads, 126 1-mm pink seed beads, nylon thread (1 100-cm length, 150-cm length)

Instructions

(1) String an amazonite bead on center of nylon thread; run both ends of thread through motif, forming an intersection in a round glass bead (A).

(2) Make band; tie threads together, hide ends in beads and cut excess (B).

Amazonite bead

Glass bead (pink)

★

A

B Back view

Fire-polished bead

1 2 3 4 5 6 7 8   12 13

NECKLACE

Supplies

14 6-mm round amazonite beads, 15 pink and 15 bronze 4-mm round glass beads, 193 bronze 3-mm round glass beads, 621 pink 1-mm seed beads, 2 crimp beads, 6-mm jump ring, spring clasp, adjustable chain closure, nylon thread (1 30-cm length, 1 100-cm length), 2 70-cm lengths nylon-coated wire

Instructions

(1) Make motif; with new thread, add an amazonite bead in center of motif (A).

(2) Insert a jump ring into edge of motif; pass nylon-coated wire through jump ring (B); string beads on wire.

(3) Attach a crimp bead to each end, then clasp and adjustable chain closure.

A

Amazonite bead

B

Clasp

Crimp bead

Adjustable chain closure

a(12)

a(11)

a(10)

a(9)

a(8)

a(7)

a(6)

a(5)

a(4)

Amazonite bead

a(3)

a(2)

4-mm glass bead (bronze)

Glass bead (pink)

a(1)

6 3-mm glass beads (bronze)

495 1-mm seed beads

Jump ring

21

PURE DOME

We used button-shaped beads and cool colors for an uncomplicated, tranquil effect.

MOTIF5

PURE DOME

This is a calm, crisp motif worked in sherbet colors. The dome shape enhances its three-dimensional aspect. The bicone and amazonite beads peeking out here and there add interest. Instructions: p. 24

BRACELET

Button-shaped beads accent the band of this bracelet, woven in the flower stitch. Instructions: p. 25.

RING

Milky white-yellow beads on the band harmonize with the largish motif for an ethereal look. Instructions: p. 24.

NECKLACE

Beads of different shapes, for instance bicone and button beads, are the accents in this necklace, which echoes the pattern of the motif. Instructions are on p.25.

23

(1) String beads on center of 100cm nylon thread; form an intersection in a button bead (A).

(2) Weave beads on nylon thread (A).

(3) Form an intersection in a button bead (B).

(4) Close circle, forming an intersection in a bicone bead.

(5) String amazonite beads, picking up bicone and button beads on perimeter of motif (C).

(6) Form an intersection in first amazonite bead strung (C).

(7) Pull threads tightly to form the dome.

(8) Add amazonite and button beads, picking up bicone beads on perimeter (D).

(9) String bicone beads on one side of thread; tie threads together, hide ends in beads and cut excess (D).

A

Amazonite bead
Button bead
Bicone bead
★ 3-mm bicone bead

B

Bicone bead

C

Amazonite bead

D

3 amazonite beads
Button bead

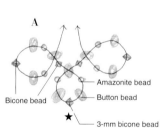

RING

Supplies

8 green 3-mm bicone crystal beads, 16 milky white-yellow 4 x 7-mm designer button beads, 80 2-mm round amazonite beads, nylon thread (1 50-cm length, 1 100-cm length)

Instructions

(1) Pass thread through button bead in motif; weave beads as shown in drawing.

(2) Tie threads together, hide in beads and cut excess.

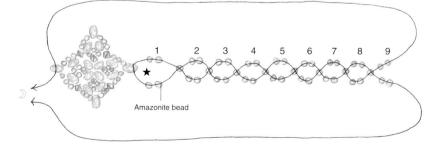

1   2   3   4   5   6   7   8   9

★
Amazonite bead

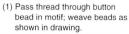

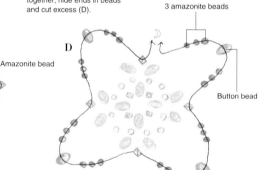

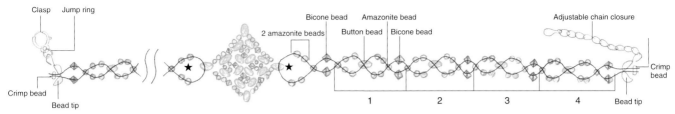

Clasp   Jump ring

Crimp bead

Bead tip

2 amazonite beads

Bicone bead

Button bead   Bicone bead

Amazonite bead

Adjustable chain closure

Crimp bead

Bead tip

1   2   3   4

BRACELET

Supplies

28 green 3-mm bicone crystal beads, 24 milky white-yellow 4 x 7-mm designer button beads, 126 2-mm round amazonite beads, 2 bead tips, 2 crimp beads, 4-mm jump ring, spring clasp, adjustable chain closure, nylon thread (2 60-cm lengths, 1 100-cm length)

Instructions

(1) Pass thread through button bead on perimeter of motif; weave left and right bands, referring to drawing.
(2) String a bead tip and crimp bead on each end of bracelet; attach clasp and adjustable chain closure.

NECKLACE

Supplies

40 green 3-mm bicone crystal beads, 14 green 4-mm bicone crystal beads, 32 milky white-yellow 4 x 7-mm designer button beads, 132 2-mm round amazonite beads, 2 crimp beads, spring clasp, adjustable chain closure, 100cm nylon thread, 60cm nylon-coated wire

Instructions

(1) String motif and additional beads on nylon-coated wire, referring to drawing.
(2) String a crimp bead on each end of necklace; attach clasp and adjustable chain closure.

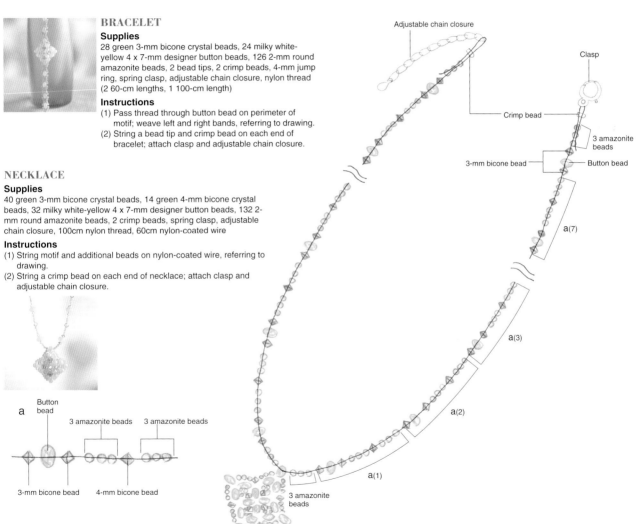

Adjustable chain closure

Clasp

Crimp bead

3 amazonite beads

3-mm bicone bead

Button bead

a(7)

a(3)

a(2)

a(1)

3 amazonite beads

a

Button bead

3 amazonite beads   3 amazonite beads

3-mm bicone bead

4-mm bicone bead

DIAMOND FLOWER

The sparkle of a tiny faux diamond creates a majestic aura.

EARRINGS

To make these earrings, we attached motifs to perforated earring backs. The faux diamonds shimmer brilliantly. Instructions: p. 29.

NECKLACE

Here we attached the motif to a perforated finding, which hangs from a chain for a beautiful effect. Instructions: p. 29.

RING

This piece was designed to make a perfect pair with the necklace. The bronze beads in the band give it an antique feel. Instructions: p. 28.

MOTIF6

DIAMOND FLOWER

This small (1.5mm in diameter) motif was designed to accentuate the faux diamond at its center. The rhodonite beads add extra elegance. In all three pieces, the motif is the uncontested star. Instructions: p. 28.

(1) String faux diamond and fire-polished beads on 80cm nylon thread; form an intersection in round fire-polished bead (A).

(2) Form an intersection in fire-polished bead without passing thread through hole in diamond bead (B).

(3) Pass thread through hole in diamond bead; form an intersection in fire-polished bead (B).

(4) Repeat Steps (2) and (3); form an intersection in first fire-polished bead strung (B).

(5) String rhodonite beads on thread, picking up blue fire-polished beads as you go along, and add another layer (C).

(6) This is how motif should look after two layers have been added (C).

(7) Work the layered stitch for one round, then set one end of thread aside (C).

(8) String bicone beads on other end of thread, picking up bronze fire-polished beads as you go along.

(9) After making one round of motif, pass thread through first blue fire-polished bead strung; tie to other end of thread, hide ends in beads and cut excess thread (D).

A

[Diamond] bead

★

Fire-polished bead (bronze)   Fire-polished bead (blue)

B

★

C

Set aside.

Rhodonite bead

D

Bicone bead

RING

Supplies

8 2-mm round rhodonite beads, 12 bronze 3-mm bicone crystal beads, 8 blue and 18 bronze 3-mm round fire-polished beads, 9 bronze 1.8-mm 3-cut beads, 6-mm diamond bead in 4-pronged mounting, nylon thread (1 80-cm length, 1 50cm length)

Instructions

(1) Make motif; pass new length of thread through motif; make band, referring to drawing.
(2) Tie threads together, hide ends in beads and cut excess.

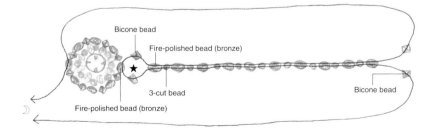

Bicone bead

Fire-polished bead (bronze)

★

3-cut bead

Fire-polished bead (bronze)

Bicone bead

EARRINGS

Supplies

16 2-mm round rhodonite beads, 16 bronze 3-mm bicone crystal beads, 16 each blue and bronze 3-mm round fire-polished beads, 2 6-mm rhinestones in 4-pronged mountings, 13-mm perforated earring backs (post style), nylon thread (2 50-cm lengths, 2 80-cm lengths)

Instructions

(1) Baste motif to four locations on perforated earring back (A and B).
(2) Cut tabs on earring back in half; bend tabs down with flat-nose pliers to secure motif.

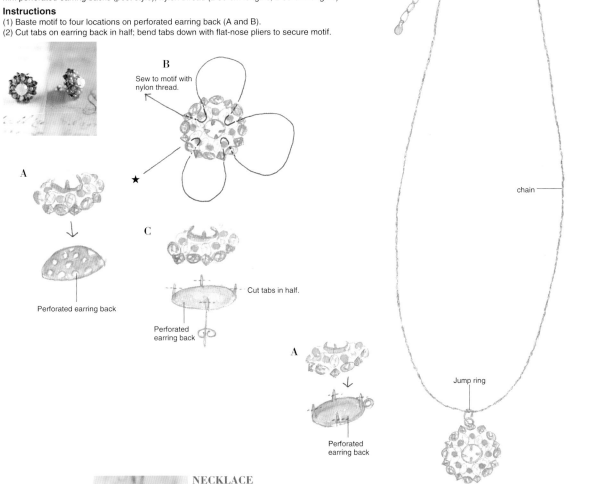

B

Sew to motif with nylon thread.

★

A

Perforated earring back

C

Cut tabs in half.

Perforated earring back

A

Perforated earring back

B

Clasp

Jump ring

Adjustable chain closure

chain

Jump ring

NECKLACE

Supplies

8 2-mm round rhodonite beads, 8 bronze 3-mm bicone crystal beads, 8 each blue and bronze 3-mm round fire-polished beads, 6-mm milky white rhinestone in 4-pronged mounting, 3 4-mm jump rings, 42cm chain, 13-mm perforated necklace finding, spring clasp, adjustable chain closure, nylon thread (1 30-cm length, 1 80-cm length)

Instructions

(1) Make motif; attach motif to base of perforated finding, referring to A and following instructions for earrings.
(2) Attach a jump ring to link at top of perforated finding; pass chain through jump ring.
(3) Attach clasp to one end and adjustable chain closure to other (B).

CROWN

A brilliant diadem truly fit for a queen!

NECKLACE

To make this necklace, we attached two lengths of chain to the motif with a wire coil and a jump ring. Instructions: p. 33

BROOCH

Here the motif and a length of chain studded with metal charms and bicone beads adorn a kilt pin. Instructions: p. 33

CELL PHONE STRAP

We've kept this strap design simple, adding just a few beads and some chain, since the motif is so distinctive. Instructions: p. 33

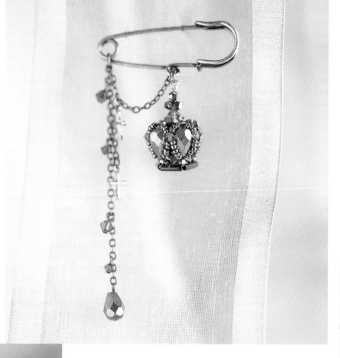

MOTIF7
CROWN

We turned five teardrop beads upside down, and lo and behold, we had made a tiny crown! The base is made from bugle beads, and seed, bicone and smaller teardrop beads are the crown jewels. Instructions: p. 32

31

(1) String bugle beads on center of 100cm nylon thread; form an intersection to close circle.

(2) String a 4-mm bicone bead and 3-cut beads, forming an intersection in a 3-cut bead (B).

(3) Pass thread through a bugle bead, then add a 4-mm bicone bead and a 3-cut bead, forming an intersection in 3-cut bead (B).

(4) At end of first round, form an intersection in a 4-mm bicone bead (B).

(5) String teardrop, 3-cut and 3-mm bicone beads on each end of nylon thread (C).

(6) Form an intersection in teardrop, 3-cut and 3-mm bicone bead on one end of thread (C).

(7) Repeat (6); form an intersection in teardrop bead only (C).

(8) Insert central teardrop bead into cluster of teardrop beads.

(9) Add seed and 3-mm bicone beads to teardrop beads (D).

(10) Add another row of beads (D).

(11) Tie threads together, hide ends in beads and cut excess (D).

(12) Pass a separate 30-cm length nylon thread through central teardrop bead and a 3-cut bead; tie ends together, hide in beads and cut excess (E).

A

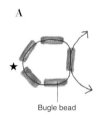

Bugle bead

B

3-cut bead

4-mm bicone bead (bronze)

C

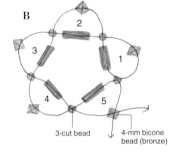

3-mm bicone bead (bronze)
3-cut bead
8
8 x 6-mm teardrop bead
9
7
7 x 5-mm teardrop bead
10
6

D

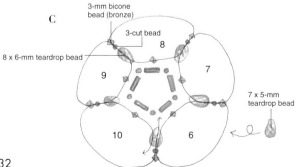

3-mm bicone bead (green)
5 seed beads
5 seed beads
3 seed beads
3 seed beads

E

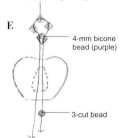

3-mm bicone bead (bronze)
4-mm bicone bead (purple)
3-cut bead

Components

a (Make 2.) 2.5cm chain

b (Make 1.) 6cm chain

c (Make 1.) Headpin — 3-mm bicone bead (bronze)

d (Make 1.) 3-mm bicone bead (green)

e (Make 1.) 4-mm bicone bead (bronze)

f (Make 1.) 4-mm bicone bead (purple)

g (Make 1.) 8 x 6-cm teardrop bead

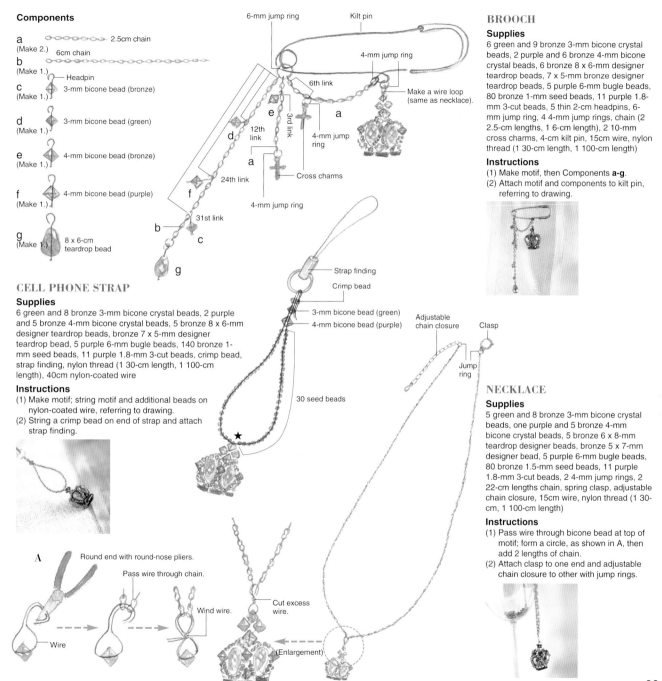

6-mm jump ring

Kilt pin

4-mm jump ring

6th link

Make a wire loop (same as necklace).

e — 3rd link

d — 12th link

a

a

24th link

f

4-mm jump ring

Cross charms

4-mm jump ring

b — 31st link

c

g

Strap finding

Crimp bead

3-mm bicone bead (green)

4-mm bicone bead (purple)

30 seed beads

Adjustable chain closure

Clasp

Jump ring

BROOCH

Supplies

6 green and 9 bronze 3-mm bicone crystal beads, 2 purple and 6 bronze 4-mm bicone crystal beads, 6 bronze 8 x 6-mm designer teardrop beads, 7 x 5-mm bronze designer teardrop beads, 5 purple 6-mm bugle beads, 80 bronze 1-mm seed beads, 11 purple 1.8-mm 3-cut beads, 5 thin 2-cm headpins, 6-mm jump ring, 4 4-mm jump rings, chain (2 2.5-cm lengths, 1 6-cm length), 2 10-mm cross charms, 4-cm kilt pin, 15cm wire, nylon thread (1 30-cm length, 1 100-cm length)

Instructions

(1) Make motif, then Components **a-g**.
(2) Attach motif and components to kilt pin, referring to drawing.

CELL PHONE STRAP

Supplies

6 green and 8 bronze 3-mm bicone crystal beads, 2 purple and 5 bronze 4-mm bicone crystal beads, 5 bronze 8 x 6-mm designer teardrop beads, bronze 7 x 5-mm designer teardrop bead, 5 purple 6-mm bugle beads, 140 bronze 1-mm seed beads, 11 purple 1.8-mm 3-cut beads, crimp bead, strap finding, nylon thread (1 30-cm length, 1 100-cm length), 40cm nylon-coated wire

Instructions

(1) Make motif; string motif and additional beads on nylon-coated wire, referring to drawing.
(2) String a crimp bead on end of strap and attach strap finding.

NECKLACE

Supplies

5 green and 8 bronze 3-mm bicone crystal beads, one purple and 5 bronze 4-mm bicone crystal beads, 5 bronze 6 x 8-mm teardrop designer beads, bronze 5 x 7-mm designer bead, 5 purple 6-mm bugle beads, 80 bronze 1.5-mm seed beads, 11 purple 1.8-mm 3-cut beads, 2 4-mm jump rings, 2 22-cm lengths chain, spring clasp, adjustable chain closure, 15cm wire, nylon thread (1 30-cm, 1 100-cm length)

Instructions

(1) Pass wire through bicone bead at top of motif; form a circle, as shown in A, then add 2 lengths of chain.
(2) Attach clasp to one end and adjustable chain closure to other with jump rings.

A Round end with round-nose pliers.

Pass wire through chain.

Wind wire.

Wire

Cut excess wire.

(Enlargement)

ELEGANT PEARLS

This design gives lustrous pearls an updated look.

RING

We designed a simple but substantial band to harmonize with the motif. To make it, all you need to do is weave figure eights. Instructions: p. 36

NECKLACE

Pearl beads serve as accents on this two-strand necklace, which looks especially beautiful when paired with darker colors. Instructions: p. 37

MOTIF8

ELEGANT PEARLS

This motif features an abundance of pearl beads (freshwater pearl beads and mother-of-pearl beads) on a coin-shaped shell bead base. We decided on a look that is almost monochrome, in keeping with our elegance theme. Instructions: p. 36

BRACELET

The band of this bracelet is built around faux leather cord, which goes amazingly well with pearl beads. Wear this in autumn or winter. Instructions: p. 37

(1) String seed beads and pearl beads on the center of 100cm nylon thread; form an intersection in a pearl bead (A).

(2) Add more beads, forming intersections in pearl beads (B).

(3) After forming 11 intersections, tie threads, hide in beads and cut excess.

(4) String 2 pearl beads on new 30-cm length nylon thread, then string a shell bead (C).

(5) Form an intersection in a pearl bead in motif (C).

(6) Add seed beads and a mother-of-pearl bead to form center of motif (D).

(7) String more seed beads; form an intersection in a pearl bead (D).

(8) Form an intersection in a pearl bead on perimeter of motif; pass one end of thread through a pearl on back of motif (D).

(9) Bring thread out on front of motif; tie threads together (D).

(10) This is how back of motif should look.

A Freshwater pearl bead

Seed bead   Seed bead

B

C   Freshwater pearl bead   Shell bead

D   Freshwater pearl bead   To front of motif   To back of motif   Seed bead   8-mm mother-of-pearl bead

RING

Supplies

32 brown 3.5-mm round freshwater pearl beads, 8-mm round mother-of-pearl bead, 30-mm coin-shaped shell bead, 26 bronze 3-mm round fire-polished beads, 24 purple 2-mm seed beads, nylon thread (1 each 30-cm, 70-cm and 100-cm lengths)

Instructions

(1) Make motif; insert new nylon thread into pearl bead on back of motif, and weave band as shown in drawings.

(2) Insert thread into other pearl bead on back of motif; tie threads together, hide ends in beads and cut excess thread.

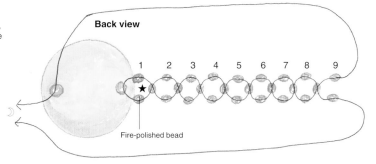

Back view

1 2 3 4 5 6 7 8 9

Fire-polished bead

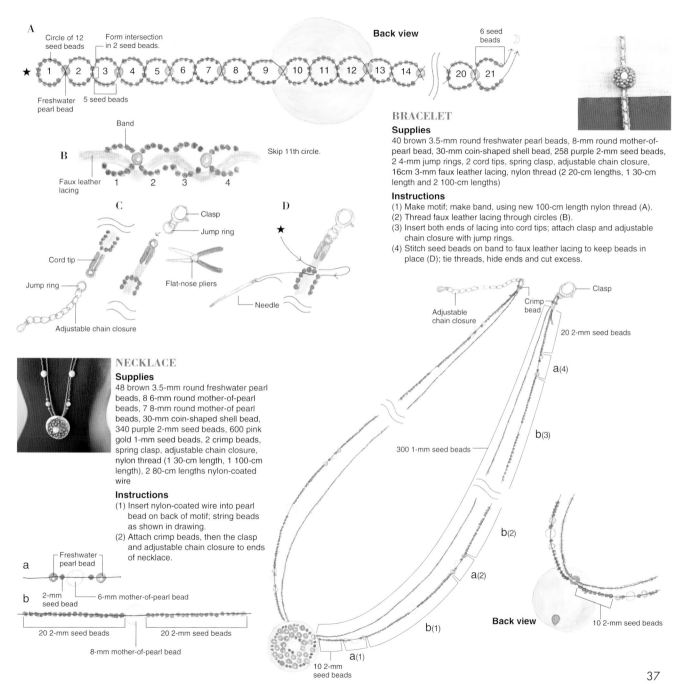

A

Circle of 12 seed beads

Form intersection in 2 seed beads.

Back view

6 seed beads

★ 1 2 3 4 5 6 7 8 9 10 11 12 13 14 20 21

Freshwater pearl bead

5 seed beads

B

Band

Skip 11th circle.

Faux leather lacing 1 2 3 4

C

Clasp

Jump ring

Cord tip

Jump ring

Flat-nose pliers

Adjustable chain closure

D

★

Needle

BRACELET

Supplies

40 brown 3.5-mm round freshwater pearl beads, 8-mm round mother-of-pearl bead, 30-mm coin-shaped shell bead, 258 purple 2-mm seed beads, 2 4-mm jump rings, 2 cord tips, spring clasp, adjustable chain closure, 16cm 3-mm faux leather lacing, nylon thread (2 20-cm lengths, 1 30-cm length and 2 100-cm lengths)

Instructions

(1) Make motif; make band, using new 100-cm length nylon thread (A).
(2) Thread faux leather lacing through circles (B).
(3) Insert both ends of lacing into cord tips; attach clasp and adjustable chain closure with jump rings.
(4) Stitch seed beads on band to faux leather lacing to keep beads in place (D); tie threads, hide ends and cut excess.

NECKLACE

Supplies

48 brown 3.5-mm round freshwater pearl beads, 8 6-mm round mother-of-pearl beads, 7 8-mm round mother-of pearl beads, 30-mm coin-shaped shell bead, 340 purple 2-mm seed beads, 600 pink gold 1-mm seed beads, 2 crimp beads, spring clasp, adjustable chain closure, nylon thread (1 30-cm length, 1 100-cm length), 2 80-cm lengths nylon-coated wire

Instructions

(1) Insert nylon-coated wire into pearl bead on back of motif; string beads as shown in drawing.
(2) Attach crimp beads, then the clasp and adjustable chain closure to ends of necklace.

a

Freshwater pearl bead

b

2-mm seed bead

6-mm mother-of-pearl bead

20 2-mm seed beads

20 2-mm seed beads

8-mm mother-of-pearl bead

Adjustable chain closure

Crimp bead

Clasp

20 2-mm seed beads

a(4)

300 1-mm seed beads

b(3)

b(2)

a(2)

b(1)

a(1)

10 2-mm seed beads

Back view

10 2-mm seed beads

37

TYPES OF BEADS

Beads come in an amazing variety of shapes and sizes — that is one of their main attractions.
On this page we introduce some of the beads used for the projects in this book.

【Seed beads】 These are probably the beads you'll see most often.

2-mm seed beads

3-mm seed beads

1-mm seed beads

【3-cut beads】
These beads, with their irregularly cut surfaces, sparkle in the light. They are available in the same range of sizes as seed beads.

【Designer beads】 These are distinctive beads, made out of every imaginable material, from plastic to gemstones.

Teardrop beads　　**Oval beads**　　**Cat's-eye bead**　　**Button-shaped beads**

3-mm beads

【Faceted glass beads】 The facets (cuts) on the surface are the reason why these beads reflect light so beautifully. They are usually classified by shape.

Bicone beads　　**Round beads**　　**Fire-polished beads**　　**Spacer beads**

6-mm beads

【Bugle beads】
These tubular beads come in several sizes, of which the 3-mm and 6-mm beads are very popular.

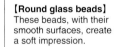

【Pearl beads】
These are usually glass beads processed to make them look like pearls. They have larger holes than freshwater pearl beads.

【Round glass beads】
These beads, with their smooth surfaces, create a soft impression.

【Metal beads, charms and connectors】
These components, usually silver or gold-plated, lend a relaxed note to a piece of jewelry. They are available in a huge spectrum of styles.

【Mounted stones】
Incorporate a mounted faux diamond or gemstone into an article of jewelry for a luxurious look.

PART 2

VARIATIONS ON A THEME

These are variations not in pattern or structure, but in the colors and types of beads used. You can make two rings, for instance, following the same instructions, but when you vary the beads, results will be surprisingly different! Choose your favorite beads and favorite colors, and create a unique piece of jewelry.

VARIATION 1
DROP NECKLACES AND RINGS

Candy-colored teardrop designer beads form the center of the necklace, and tiny seed beads provide accents. The yellow-orange version featuring carnelian beads will brighten anybody's day. The pink version featuring rose quartz beads makes a subtler impression.

RING 1: CARNELIAN RING

Supplies

12 10 x 6-mm teardrop carnelian beads, 43 2-mm round gold sandstone beads, 18 bronze 1-mm seed beads, nylon thread (1 60-cm length, 1 80-cm length)

RING 2: ROSE QUARTZ RING

Supplies

12 10 x 7-mm teardrop rose quartz beads, 43 pink 2-mm round coral beads, 18 pink 1-mm seed beads, nylon thread (1 60-cm length, 1 80-cm length)

Instructions*

(1) String beads, referring to Drawing A.
(2) Add 1-mm seed beads, picking up beads on perimeter (B); tie threads together, hide ends in beads and cut excess.
(3) Weave band, referring to Drawing C; tie threads together, hide ends in beads and cut excess.

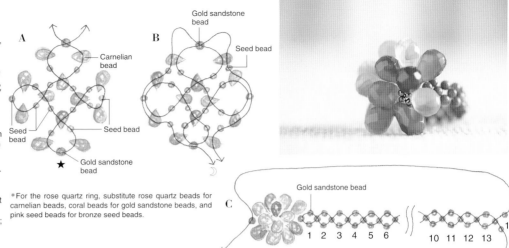

A

Carnelian bead

Seed bead

Seed bead

Gold sandstone bead

B

Gold sandstone bead

Seed bead

*For the rose quartz ring, substitute rose quartz beads for carnelian beads, coral beads for gold sandstone beads, and pink seed beads for bronze seed beads.

C
Gold sandstone bead
1 2 3 4 5 6   10 11 12 13 14

NECKLACE 1: CARNELIAN NECKLACE

Supplies

12 10 x 6-mm teardrop carnelian beads, 44 4-mm round carnelian beads, 22 6 x 3-mm button orange moonstone beads, 77 2-mm round gold sandstone beads, 106 bronze 1-mm seed beads, 2 crimp beads, spring clasp, adjustable chain closure, 60cm nylon thread, 80cm nylon-coated wire

NECKLACE 2: ROSE QUARTZ NECKLACE

Supplies

12 10 x 7-mm teardrop rose quartz beads, 44 4-mm round rose quartz beads, 22 8 x 3-mm button rose quartz beads, 77 pink 2-mm round coral beads, 106 pink 1-mm seed beads, 2 crimp beads, spring clasp, adjustable chain closure, 60cm nylon thread, 80cm nylon-coated wire

Instructions*

(1) Make motif, following instructions for rings above.
(2) Pass nylon-coated wire (centered) through motif ; form an intersection as shown in drawing.
(3) Repeat pattern (see drawing below) 11 times; attach a crimp bead to each end of necklace, then clasp or adjustable chain closure.

*For rose quartz necklace, make substitutions indicated for ring.

Pattern for Necklace 2

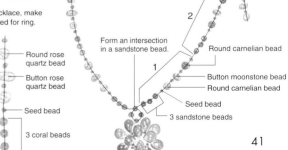

Adjustable chain closure

Clasp

Crimp bead

3 sandstone beads

11

2

Form an intersection in a sandstone bead.

Round carnelian bead

Round rose quartz bead

Button rose quartz bead

Seed bead

3 coral beads

1

Button moonstone bead

Round carnelian bead

Seed bead

3 sandstone beads

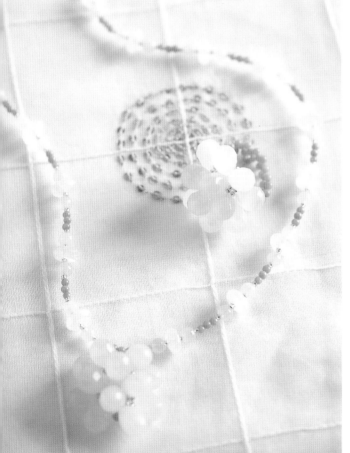

41

VARIATION 2
CROSS BRACELETS

We made two versions of the same bracelet in black and silver. In the black bracelet, we used pink rhodonite beads for contrast. In the other version, we paired silver beads with lustrous mother-of-pearl beads.

BRACELET 1: SILVER BRACELET

Supplies

10 6-mm round mother-of-pearl beads, 8 white 3-mm bicone crystal beads, 324 silver 1-mm seed beads, 2 bead tips, 2 crimp beads, 4-mm jump ring, spring clasp, adjustable chain closure, nylon thread (2 50-cm lengths, 1 80-cm length)

BRACELET 2: BLACK BRACELET

Supplies

10 6-mm round rhodonite beads, 8 black 3-mm bicone crystal beads, 324 black 1-mm seed beads, 2 bead tips, 2 crimp beads, 4-mm jump ring, spring clasp, adjustable chain closure, nylon thread (2 50-cm lengths, 1 80-cm length)

Instructions*

(1) String beads, referring to A.
(2) Weave figure eights as shown in B; form intersection in mother-of-pearl bead, then set one length of thread aside.
(3) Add seed beads, picking up mother-of-pearl and seed beads on perimeter (C); after completing one round, tie to length of thread previously set aside.
(4) With separate thread, weave as shown in D, picking up seed beads on motif and working left and right sides in mirror image.
(5) String a bead tip and crimp bead on each end of bracelet; compress crimp beads, close bead tips; attach clasp to one end and adjustable chain closure to other.

*For black bracelet, simply substitute beads listed under Supplies.

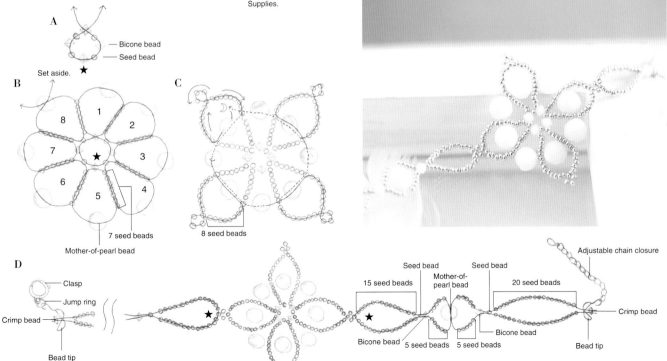

A
— Bicone bead
— Seed bead
Set aside. ★

B
8 1 2
7 ★ 3
6 5 4
7 seed beads
Mother-of-pearl bead

C
8 seed beads

D
Clasp
Jump ring
Crimp bead
Bead tip

★ ★
Bicone bead
15 seed beads
5 seed beads
5 seed beads
Seed bead
Mother-of-pearl bead
Bicone bead
Seed bead
20 seed beads
Adjustable chain closure
Crimp bead
Bead tip

43

VARIATION 3
HYDRANGEA RINGS

The hydrangea blossom was the inspiration for the clusters of tiny flowers on these rings. One version reproduces actual hydrangea colors: greens, whites and lavenders. The other two color schemes are more fanciful.

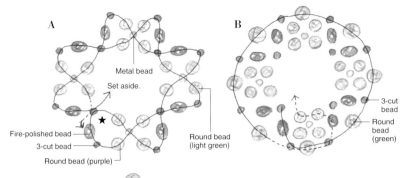

A

Metal bead

Set aside.

Fire-polished bead

3-cut bead

Round bead (purple)

B

3-cut bead

Round bead (green)

C

Metal bead

Round bead (white)

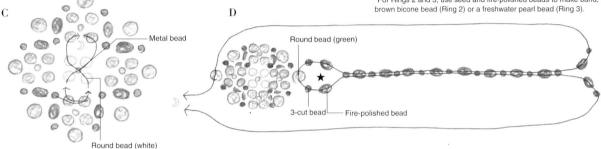

D

Round bead (green)

3-cut bead — Fire-polished bead

RING 1: GREEN RING

Supplies
4 white, 8 purple and 8 light green 4-mm round beads, 20 iridescent green 3-mm round fire-polished beads, 5 silver 2-mm round metal beads, 25 iridescent green 1.8-mm 3-cut beads, nylon thread (1 30-cm length, 1 70-cm length)

Instructions*
(1) Weave a circle, referring to A, and ending by forming an intersection in first 3-cut bead strung; set one length of nylon thread aside.
(2) Add 4-mm green beads, picking up 3-cut beads on perimeter of motif; after working one round, bring thread out at center of motif (B).
(3) String white 4-mm round and metal beads on thread previously set aside (C); tie threads together, hide ends in beads and cut excess.
(4) Using separate thread, make band; tie threads together, hide ends in beads and cut excess (D).

*For Rings 2 and 3, use seed and fire-polished beads to make band, picking up a brown bicone bead (Ring 2) or a freshwater pearl bead (Ring 3).

RING 2: BROWN RING

Supplies
4 light pink, 8 pink, 8 light brown and 8 brown 4-mm bicone crystal beads, 20 brown 3-mm round fire-polished beads, 5 silver 2-mm round metal beads, 25 brown 2-mm seed beads, nylon thread (1 60-cm length, 1 70-cm length)

RING 3: NATURAL STONE

Supplies
4 4-mm round blue lace agate beads, 8 4-mm round rhodonite beads, 8 4-mm round amazonite beads, 8 white 4-mm round freshwater pearl beads, 20 pink gold 3-mm round fire-polished beads, 5 silver 2-mm round metal beads, 25 pink 2-mm seed beads, nylon thread (1 60-cm length, 1 70-cm length)

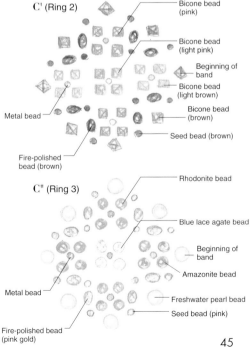

C' (Ring 2)

Bicone bead (pink)

Bicone bead (light pink)

Beginning of band

Bicone bead (light brown)

Bicone bead (brown)

Seed bead (brown)

Metal bead

Fire-polished bead (brown)

C" (Ring 3)

Rhodonite bead

Blue lace agate bead

Beginning of band

Amazonite bead

Freshwater pearl bead

Seed bead (pink)

Metal bead

Fire-polished bead (pink gold)

45

VARIATION 4
POP FLOWER RINGS

You're bound to fall in love with these cheerful flower rings with their layered petals worked in two colors. The red ring is made from round coral beads, while the white and blue rings feature bicone beads.

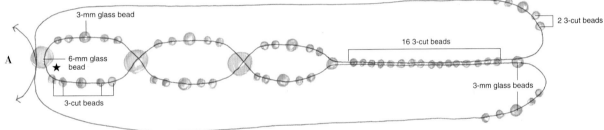

A

- 3-mm glass bead
- 6-mm glass bead ★
- 3-cut beads
- 16 3-cut beads
- 2 3-cut beads
- 3-mm glass beads

RING 1: WHITE RING

Supplies

30 white 3-mm bicone crystal beads, 10 bronze 3-mm round glass beads, 3 brown 6-mm round glass beads, 48 bronze 1.8-mm 3-cut beads, 80 cm nylon thread

RING 2: BLUE RING

Supplies

30 blue 3-mm bicone crystal beads, 10 green 3-mm round glass beads, 3 light green 6-mm round glass beads, 46 green 2-mm seed beads, 80cm nylon thread

RING 3: RED RING

Supplies

10 red and 30 pink 2-mm round coral beads, 10 red 3-mm round coral beads, 3 red 5-mm round coral beads, 80 cm nylon thread

Instructions*

(1) String beads on center of nylon thread, referring to A; form an intersection in first glass bead strung.

(2) Weave bicone beads onto 6-mm round glass beads; tie threads together, hide ends in beads and cut excess.

*For blue ring, substitute 2-mm seed beads for 3-cut beads; for band, substitute 14 seed beads for 16 3-cut beads. For the red ring, follow instructions in BN; to shorten ring, subtract red 2-mm coral beads; for band, substitute 12 red 2-mm coral beads for 16 3-cut beads.

B

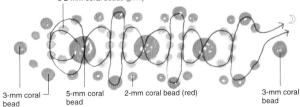

5 bicone beads

B' (red ring)

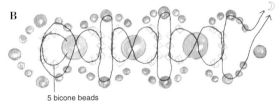

5 2-mm coral beads (pink)

- 3-mm coral bead
- 5-mm coral bead
- 2-mm coral bead (red)
- 3-mm coral bead

47

VARIATION 5
WAVE BRACELETS

By alternating the positions of beads, we created a
bracelet reminiscent of a series of waves. If you make
either of the variations, you'll find it hard to believe that
you're looking at the same design!

BRACELET 1: PEARL BRACELET

Supplies

Blue-gray 6-mm round freshwater pearl bead, 76 blue-gray 4 x 3-mm top-drilled freshwater pearl beads, 77 2-mm round blue sandstone beads, 173 black 1-mm seed beads, 200cm nylon thread

BRACELET 2: FACETED-GLASS BEAD BRACELET

Supplies

Brown 8-mm round fire-polished bead, 37 orange and 38 green 4-mm round fire-polished beads, 104 pink gold 1-mm seed beads, 150cm nylon thread

Instructions for Bracelet 1*

(1) Begin weaving at center of nylon thread (A).
(2) Continue weaving, referring to B; make clasp by stringing seed beads.

*The number of seed beads needed to make the clasp will depend on the size of the freshwater pearl beads. Make the necessary adjustments. For a sturdier clasp, run thread through seed beads twice.

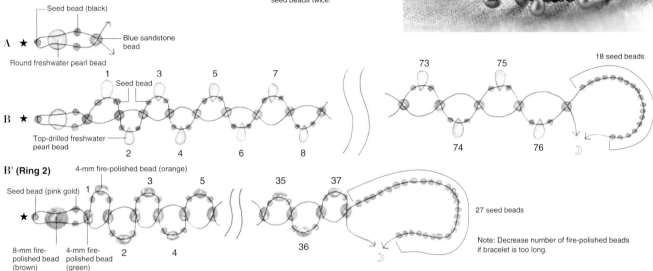

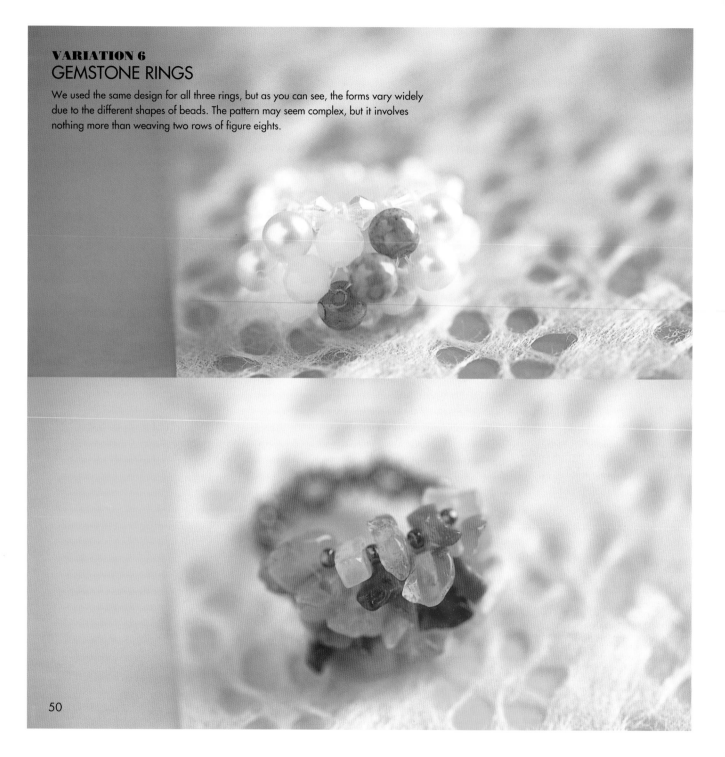

VARIATION 6
GEMSTONE RINGS

We used the same design for all three rings, but as you can see, the forms vary widely
due to the different shapes of beads. The pattern may seem complex, but it involves
nothing more than weaving two rows of figure eights.

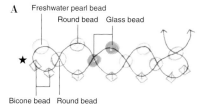

A

Freshwater pearl bead
Round bead
Glass bead

★

Bicone bead   Round bead

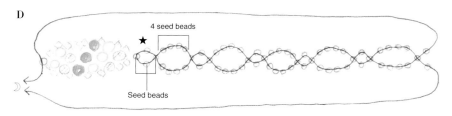

D

4 seed beads

★

Seed beads

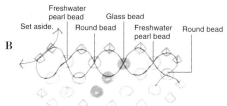

B

Set aside.
Freshwater pearl bead
Round bead
Glass bead
Freshwater pearl bead
Round bead

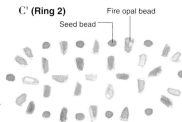

C' (Ring 2)

Seed bead   Fire opal bead

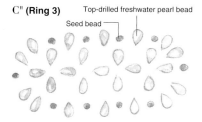

C" (Ring 3)

Seed bead   Top-drilled freshwater pearl bead

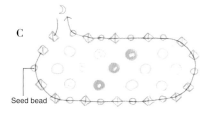

C

Seed bead

RING 1: WHITE RING

Supplies
5 white 4-mm round freshwater pearl beads, 5 white 4-mm round beads, 14 milky white 3-mm bicone crystal beads, 3 pink 4-mm round glass beads, 72 white 1-mm seed beads, nylon thread (1 60-cm length, 1 70-cm length)

RING 2: FIRE OPAL RING

Supplies
27 2-4-mm fire opal chip beads, 72 red 1-mm seed beads, nylon thread (1 60-cm length, 1 70-cm length)

RING 3: BLUE-GRAY RING

Supplies
27 blue-gray 4 x 3-mm top-drilled freshwater pearl beads, 72 black 1-mm seed beads, nylon thread (1 60-cm length, 1 70-cm length)

Instructions (Ring 1)*
(1) Weave figure eights, as shown in A.
(2) Weave Row 2 (B); form an intersection in 2 bicone beads, and set aside one end of thread.
(3) With other end of thread, add seed beads, working around perimeter and picking up bicone beads on perimeter; tie to end of thread previously set aside (C).
(4) Make band, using new thread (D); tie threads together, hide ends in beads and cut excess.

*Refer to drawings for instructions for Rings 2 and 3. For Ring 2, used fire opals only instead of beads shown in B. For Ring 3, use top-drilled freshwater pearl beads only. Use 1-mm seed beads to make bands for Rings 2 and 3.

51

VARIATION 7
SPARKLING FLOWER RINGS

With this flower motif, you can vary the
positions of the upper and lower row of petals.
Make the base, the top row and then the
bottom row of petals. This motif looks beautiful
from any angle.

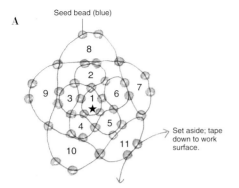

A

Seed bead (blue)

8
2
9 3 1 ★ 6 7
4 5
10 11

→ Set aside; tape down to work surface.

RING 1: BLUE RING

Supplies

Blue 6-mm round pearl bead, 6 pale blue, 7 purple and 7 blue 4-mm round fire-polished beads, 125 blue 2-mm seed beads, nylon thread (1 60-cm length, 1 100-cm length)

RING 2: PINK RING

Supplies

Brown 6-mm round pearl bead, 6 pink gold, 7 brown and 7 pearl 4-mm round fire-polished beads, 125 pink gold 2-mm seed beads, nylon thread (1 60-cm length, 1 100-cm length)

RING 3: GEMSTONE RING

Supplies

White 6-mm round freshwater pearl bead, 20 mixed 4-mm round rutile quartz beads, 125 silver 2-mm seed beads, nylon thread (1 60-cm length, 1 100-cm length)

Instructions (Ring 1)

(1) Make base of motif with seed beads, referring to A; set aside one end of thread.
(2) Make upper row of petals, picking up seed beads on perimeter (B).
(3) Make lower row of petals, repeating Step (2); tie thread to other end of thread previously set aside, hide ends in beads and cut excess (C).
(4) String pearl beads on center of new thread, then pass thread through motif; form an intersection in a seed bead on back of motif (D).
(5) Make band (E); tie threads together, hide ends in beads and cut excess.

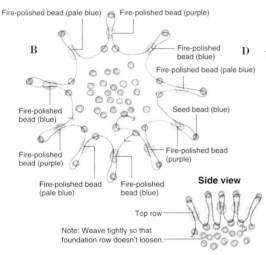

B

Fire-polished bead (pale blue)   Fire-polished bead (purple)

Fire-polished bead (blue)

Fire-polished bead (pale blue)

Fire-polished bead (blue)

Seed bead (blue)

Fire-polished bead (purple)

Fire-polished bead (purple)

Fire-polished bead (pale blue)   Fire-polished bead (blue)

Side view

Top row

Note: Weave tightly so that foundation row doesn't loosen.

D   ★   Peal bead

Seed bead

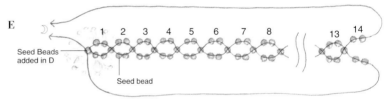

E

Seed Beads added in D

1 2 3 4 5 6 7 8   13 14

Seed bead

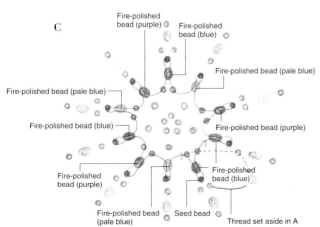

C

Fire-polished bead (purple)   Fire-polished bead (blue)

Fire-polished bead (pale blue)

Fire-polished bead (pale blue)

Fire-polished bead (blue)

Fire-polished bead (purple)

Fire-polished bead (purple)

Fire-polished bead (blue)

Fire-polished bead (pale blue)   Seed bead   Thread set aside in A

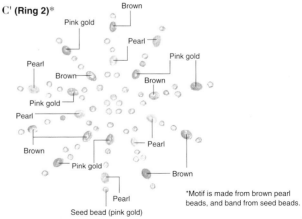

C' (Ring 2)*

Brown
Pink gold
Pearl
Pearl   Pink gold
Pearl   Brown   Brown
Pink gold
Pearl
Brown   Pearl
Pink gold
Pink gold   Brown
Pearl
Seed bead (pink gold)

*Motif is made from brown pearl beads, and band from seed beads.

53

GEMSTONE AND PEARL BEADS

Gemstone and pearl beads, which come in many shapes and sizes, add a very special richness to any piece of jewelry. We encourage you to create designs that emphasize their attributes.

Amazonite
A variety of moonstone, amazonite is said to inspire hope and confidence.

Peridot
The peridot, credited with strong healing powers, was worshiped as the "gem of the sun" in ancient Egypt.

Shell
Shell beads are, of course, made from the shells of sea animals. Most of them are white or brown, and all of them have their own special luster.

Amethyst
A stone associated with the moon goddess, and purported to have healing powers.

Orange moonstone
A type of moonstone believed to comfort the distressed.

Blue lace agate
The pale blue and white streaks in this gemstone are said to help us relax.

Pink tourmaline
Among all the different types of tourmaline, pink tourmaline symbolizes sincerity and love.

Gold sandstone
The gold in gold sandstone looks like glitter. There is also a blue sandstone.

Rose quartz
Rose quartz is a type of crystal associated with the goddess of love and beauty, and known as the comforter of the lovelorn.

Fluorite
Fluorite is found in many colors, chiefly purple and green, and is believed to increase awareness.

Labradorite
Discovered near Labrador, Canada, labradorite is valued for its iridescence. It purportedly inspires creativity.

Coral (red)
A treasure from the sea arguably as important as pearls. Red coral reportedly stimulates circulation and activity.

Coral (pink)
Pink coral is said to protect lovers. White and black are other colors of coral.

Moss agate
So called because of its resemblance to moss, this gemstone is believed to have a tranquilizing effect.

Smoky quartz
Legend has it that this gemstone, with its smoky gray color, fends off evil spirits and rejuvenates the spirit.

Mother-of-pearl
Mother-of-pearl is the base material from which a mollusk forms its shell. Its milky white color symbolizes motherhood.

Freshwater pearls
These pearls are made by mussels, whose habitat is fresh water. Freshwater pearls are often dyed green, gold and other colors.

Red agate
Agate is reputed to help boost energy. Red agate symbolizes affection, and is believed to suppress anger.

Carnelian
Carnelian, worn by both Mohammed and Napoleon, is supposed to ensure victory and success.

Olive jade
This olive-green gemstone is distinguished by tiny black flecks.

Fire opal
The name of this gemstone, usually orange or yellow, comes from its resemblance to flames. It is believed to stimulate energy.

Green aventurine
The name of this gemstone comes from the Italian word for "accidental." It is said to bring victory to anyone who wears or carries it.

Citrine
A member of the crystal family, citrine is usually lemon-colored or gold. It reportedly symbolizes prosperity.

Rutile quartz
This gemstone is quartz in which needle-shaped rutile crystals are embedded. Occurring in a variety of colors, rutile quartz is said to heighten the sensibilities.

Turquoise
Turquoise is sacred to American Indians, who believe that it promotes friendship and love, and wards off trouble.

PART 3
MORE BEAD
JEWELRY

In this section, we present individual rings, earrings and necklaces.
The designs in this collection range from the opulence of gemstones
and pearls to the mystery of Asian-inspired pieces. We also introduce
a new material, fine mesh tubing, which adds to the pleasure of
working with beads.

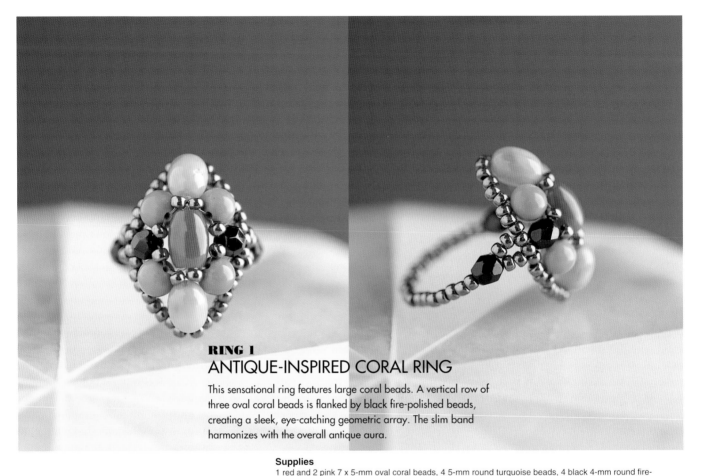

RING 1
ANTIQUE-INSPIRED CORAL RING

This sensational ring features large coral beads. A vertical row of three oval coral beads is flanked by black fire-polished beads, creating a sleek, eye-catching geometric array. The slim band harmonizes with the overall antique aura.

Supplies

1 red and 2 pink 7 x 5-mm oval coral beads, 4 5-mm round turquoise beads, 4 black 4-mm round fire-polished beads, 74 brown 2-mm seed beads, nylon thread (1 60-cm length, 1 80-cm length)

Instructions

(1) String beads as shown in A; after weaving one round, work back to a seed bead and set thread aside.
(2) Run other end of thread through seed beads on perimeter of motif; bring thread out at location shown in drawing (B).
(3) Place red coral bead at center of motif and pass both ends of thread through it, as shown in C; tie threads.
(4) With new thread, pick up two seed beads on motif, and make band (D); tie threads together, hide ends in bead and cut excess.

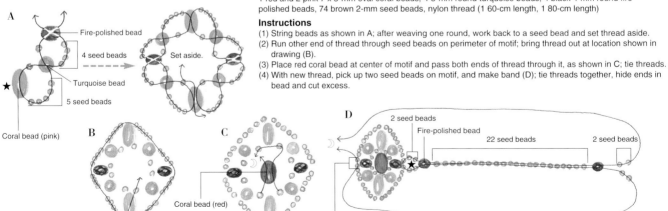

56

RING 2
RED AGATE AND TURQUOISE RING

This simple design is a happy marriage of red agate beads and turquoise bead clusters, woven horizontally. To prevent mistakes, tape the end of the nylon thread that you're not using to your work surface.

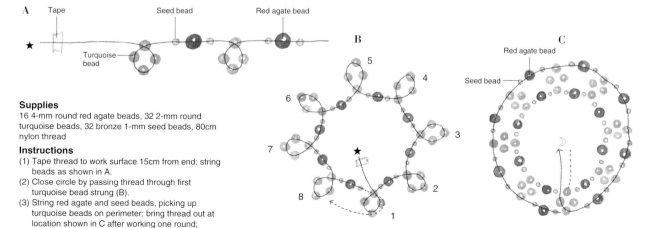

A Tape — Seed bead — Red agate bead — Turquoise bead

B

C Red agate bead — Seed bead

Supplies
16 4-mm round red agate beads, 32 2-mm round turquoise beads, 32 bronze 1-mm seed beads, 80cm nylon thread

Instructions
(1) Tape thread to work surface 15cm from end; string beads as shown in A.
(2) Close circle by passing thread through first turquoise bead strung (B).
(3) String red agate and seed beads, picking up turquoise beads on perimeter; bring thread out at location shown in C after working one round; remove tape, tie threads and cut excess.

57

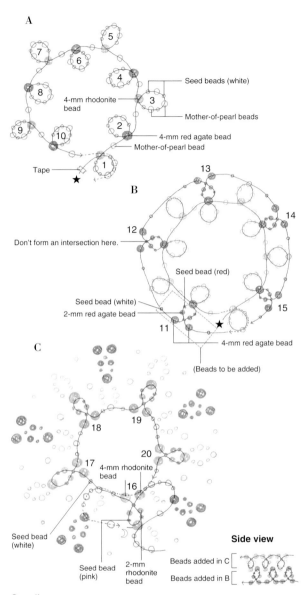

A

Seed beads (white)

4-mm rhodonite bead

Mother-of-pearl beads

4-mm red agate bead

Mother-of-pearl bead

Tape ★

B

Don't form an intersection here.

Seed bead (red)

Seed bead (white)

2-mm red agate bead

★

4-mm red agate bead

(Beads to be added)

C

4-mm rhodonite bead

Seed bead (white)

Seed bead (pink)

2-mm rhodonite bead

Side view

Beads added in C
Beads added in B

RING 3
ARGYLE RING

The inspiration for this design came from the argyle pattern often used for knitted garments. We updated this traditional pattern by using pearls and gemstones, and a modern color combination (red, pink and white).

Supplies
10 2-mm round rhodonite beads, 15 4-mm round rhodonite beads, 10 2-mm round red agate beads, 15 4-mm round red agate beads, 40 2-mm round mother-of-pearl beads, 1-mm seed beads (15 pink, 15 red, 60 white), 100cm nylon thread

Instructions
(1) Tape one end of thread to work surface; weave beads to form a circle (A).
(2) Add more beads, picking up red agate and mother-of-pearl beads strung in (1), and referring to B.
(3) Weave rhodonite sections in the same way (C); remove tape, tie threads together and cut excess.

Supplies

4 purple 7 x 5-mm teardrop designer beads, 4 9 x 6-mm blue teardrop designer beads, 1 each gold and pink 4-mm round pearl bead, 76 pink gold 2-mm seed beads, 3 60-cm lengths nylon thread

Instructions

(1) Make motif, referring to A; set one end of thread aside.
(2) With other end of thread, work twice around perimeter, picking up seed beads; tie thread to other end previously set aside (B); make this motif in two colors.
(3) Make band with new thread (C); pass one end of thread through motif, then a pearl bead, then form an intersection in a seed bead; tie threads together and cut excess.

RING 4
TEARDROP BEAD RING

Reflecting each other's colors, clear blue, gold and purple teardrop beads combine to produce a ring with an exotic, mysterious flavor.

A

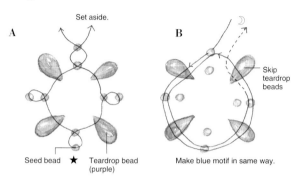

Set aside.

Seed bead ★   Teardrop bead (purple)

B

Skip teardrop beads

Make blue motif in same way.

C

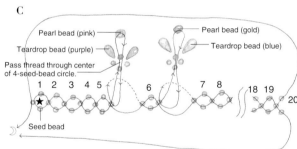

Pearl bead (pink)   Pearl bead (gold)

Teardrop bead (purple)   Teardrop bead (blue)

Pass thread through center of 4-seed-bead circle.

1 2 3 4 5   6   7 8   18 19   20

Seed bead

EARRINGS 1
CHINESE-INSPIRED EARRINGS

Bugle beads form the framework for Chinese lanterns
in these colorful earrings featuring faceted glass beads
and chain fringe.

EARRINGS 2
TASSELED EARRINGS

These earrings, also Oriental in style, are adorned
with silk thread tassels. With their perfect balance,
and the striking color combination of blue and purple,
they are sure to catch the eye.

EARRINGS 1

Supplies

2 green 5 x 3-mm spacer beads, 2 pink 3-mm bicone crystal beads, 2 iridescent blue 5-mm round fire-polished beads, 12 green 6-mm bugle beads, 6 green 2-mm seed beads, 2 2-cm thin eyepins, 6 3-cm lengths chain, ear wires, 2 50-cm lengths nylon thread

Instructions

(1) Make motif by weaving figure eights (A); tie threads and cut excess.
(2) With an awl, open the first link in each length of chain (B).
(3) Insert a fire-polished bead into center of motif; insert an eyepin into the bead and the motif; round end with round-nose pliers (C).
(4) Open other end of eyepin with flat-nose pliers; attach 3 lengths chain and ear wire (D).

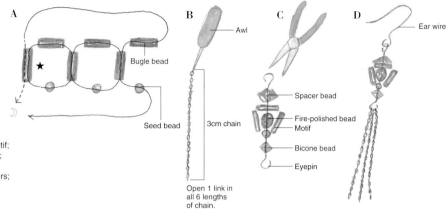

A

★

Bugle bead

Seed bead

B

Awl

Open 1 link in all 6 lengths of chain.

3cm chain

C

Spacer bead

Fire-polished bead

Motif

Bicone bead

Eyepin

D

Ear wire

EARRINGS 2

Make tassel.

Eyepin component (Make 4.)

Round bead

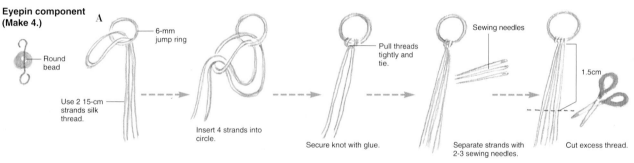

A

6-mm jump ring

Use 2 15-cm strands silk thread.

Insert 4 strands into circle.

Pull threads tightly and tie.

Secure knot with glue.

Sewing needles

Separate strands with 2-3 sewing needles.

1.5cm

Cut excess thread.

Supplies

4 turquoise 6-mm round beads, 4 2-cm thick eyepins, 4 each 4-mm and 6-mm jump rings, ear wires, 4 15-cm lengths purple silk thread, glue

Instructions

(1) Make eyepin components.
(2) Tie silk thread onto jump ring and make tassel (A).
(3) Assemble components and attach ear wire (B).

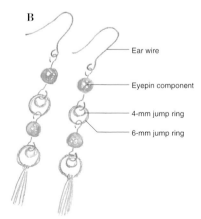

B

Ear wire

Eyepin component

4-mm jump ring

6-mm jump ring

Components

a (Make 16.)   b (Make 8.)   c (Make 2.)

Garnet bead
Headpin

Carnelian bead
Headpin

22 links (about 4cm)

Ear post
Attach to 1st link of chain

Jump ring

Jump ring

a   a   b   a   a   b

Butterfly nut (half of ear post)

a   b   a   a   b   a

Attach to jump ring.

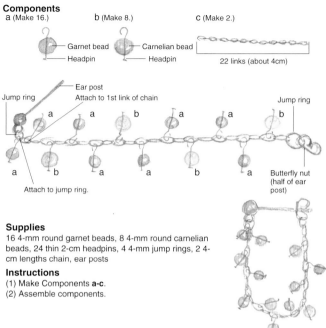

Supplies
16 4-mm round garnet beads, 8 4-mm round carnelian beads, 24 thin 2-cm headpins, 4 4-mm jump rings, 2 4-cm lengths chain, ear posts

Instructions
(1) Make Components **a-c**.
(2) Assemble components.

EARRINGS 3
CHAIN RING EARRINGS

This simple but clever design features circles of beads and chain hung on ear posts. The garnet and carnelian beads look as appetizing as the fruits of autumn!

Components

a (Make 2.)

8 x 7-mm freshwater pearl bead
2-cm eyepin

d (Make 2.)

6-mm bugle bead
2-cm eyepin

b (Make 4.)

4-mm freshwater pearl bead
2-cm eyepin

e (Make 4.)

Headpin
6-mm bugle bead

c (Make 2.)

Headpin
4-mm freshwater pearl bead

f (Make 2.)

Bend 3-cm eyepin.

Ear wire

Jump ring

a   f

b   b

d

e   c   e

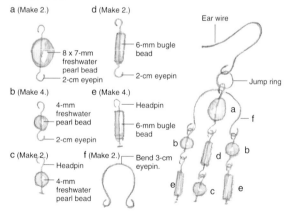

Supplies
2 light brown 8 x 7-mm freshwater pearl rice beads, 6 brown 4-mm round freshwater pearl beads, 6 bronze 6-mm bugle beads, 2 3-cm eyepins, 8 thin 2-cm eyepins, 6 2-cm thin headpins, 2 4-mm jump rings, ear wires

Instructions
(1) Make Components **a-f**.
(2) Assemble components, referring to drawings, and attach ear wires.

EARRINGS 4
CHANDELIER PEARL EARRINGS

These graceful earrings combined bugle-and-round-bead fringe suspended from curved eyepins.

EARRINGS 5 & 6
MESH TUBING EARRINGS

These earrings feature fine mesh tubing, which allows
you to stretch it to almost any shape. In these designs,
we've lined beads up vertically, sometimes enclosing
them in the tubing for an ethereal effect.

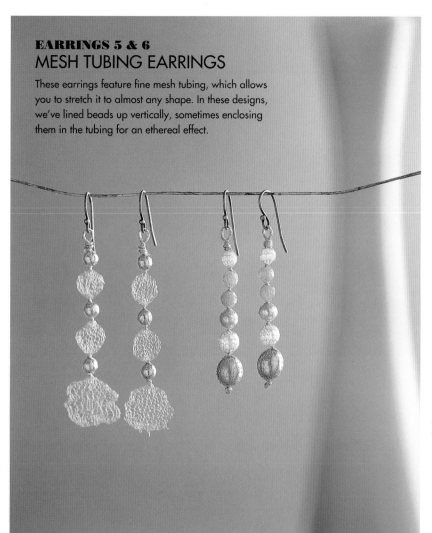

Supplies
2 4-mm round blue lace agate beads, 2 4-mm round
amazonite beads, 2 4-mm round olive jade beads, 2 pink 5-
mm round freshwater pearl beads, 2 white 6-mm round
freshwater pearl beads, 2 light brown 8 x 7-mm freshwater
pearl rice beads, 2 15-cm lengths gold 4-mm-wide mesh
tubing, ear wires

Instructions
(1) Insert gemstones into mesh tubing, as shown in drawings.
(2) Twist end of tubing, attach ear wire and wrap tubing
around base of ear wire; cut excess tubing.

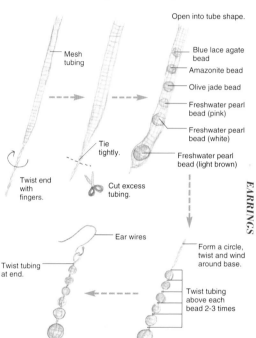

EARRINGS

EARRINGS 6:
PEARL EARRINGS

Supplies
6 gold 4-mm round pearl
beads, 2 15-cm lengths 4-mm-
wide mesh tubing, ear wires

Instructions
(1) Insert pearl beads into
mesh tubing, referring to
drawings.
(2) Twist one end of tubing,
attach ear wire and wrap
mesh tubing around base
of ear wire; cut excess
tubing.

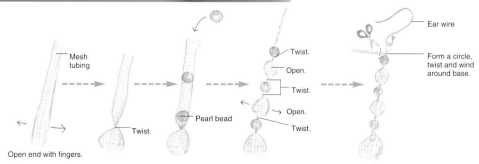

EARRINGS 7
LACY GEMSTONE HOOPS

Elegant hoop earrings are lavishly adorned with semicircular seed-bead ropes, clear pink tourmaline beads and amethyst beads.

Supplies

10 6 x 4-mm teardrop pink tourmaline beads, 12 3-mm button amethyst beads, 14 blue 4-mm round fire-polished beads, 36 light brown 2-mm seed beads, 2 4-mm hoop earring findings, 2 30-cm lengths nylon thread, glue

Instructions

(1) Weave figure eights, as shown in A; tie threads together and cut excess.
(2) String a new round fire-polished bead and the round fire-polished beads strung in (1).
(3) String a new round fire-polished bead, then glue ball to end of hoop (C).

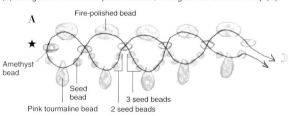

A

- Fire-polished bead
- Amethyst bead
- Seed bead
- Pink tourmaline bead
- 3 seed beads
- 2 seed beads

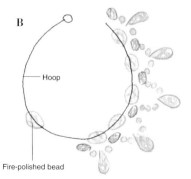

B

- Hoop
- Fire-polished bead

C

- Glue to ball.

EARRINGS 8
EARRINGS WITH METAL FRINGE

We attached metal beads of different sizes to lengths of chain, then wrapped wire around the hoops for a very modern, striking effect.

Components

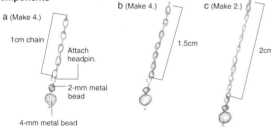

a (Make 4.)
1cm chain
Attach headpin.
2-mm metal bead
4-mm metal bead

b (Make 4.)
1.5cm

c (Make 2.)
2cm

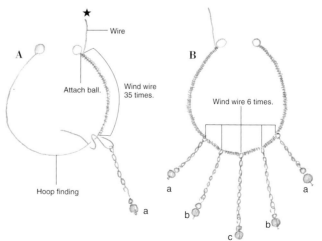

★ Wire

A
Attach ball.
Wind wire 35 times.
Hoop finding
a

B
Wind wire 6 times.
a
a
b
b
c

Supplies
10 each 2-mm and 4-mm round metal beads, 10 thin 2-cm headpins, chain (4 1-cm lengths, 4 1.5-cm lengths), 17-mm hoop earring findings, 2 100-cm lengths wire, glue

Instructions
(1) Make Components **a-c** by attaching metal beads strung on headpins to lengths of chain.
(2) Attach ball to end of hoop finding with glue; wrap wire around hoop 35 times, attach **a** and wrap wire 6 times (A).
(3) Referring to B, add remaining components, spacing them attractively among the wound wire; wind wire tightly at end of hoop to secure, and cut excess.

65

BRACELET 1
3-STRAND CORAL BRACELET

We used many sizes and shapes of coral beads to create a bracelet with real impact. The bead-ball accents would make gorgeous earrings.

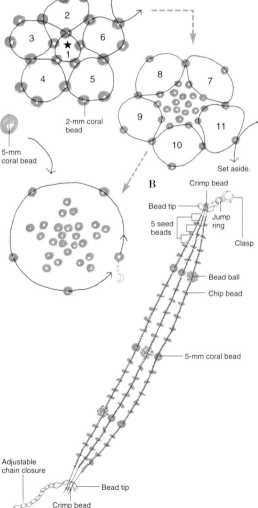

Supplies

90 red 2-mm round coral beads, 9 red 5-mm round coral beads, 54 red 5-mm chip coral beads, 330 red 1-mm seed beads, 2 bead tips, 2 crimp beads, spring clasp, adjustable chain closure, 6 40-cm lengths nylon thread

Instructions

(1) Make a bead ball from 2-mm coral beads, referring to A; when you reach 11, set one end of thread aside.

(2) With other end of thread, pick up coral beads on perimeter and enclose 5-mm coral bead; tie thread to end previously set aside (make 3 of these).

(3) String beads and bead balls on three lengths of nylon thread; attach clasp to one end of bracelet and adjustable chain closure to other end (B).

A   Make a bead ball.

2

3

★ 1

6

4

5

2-mm coral bead

8

7

9

11

10

Set aside.

5-mm coral bead

B

Crimp bead

Bead tip

5 seed beads

Jump ring

Clasp

Bead ball

Chip bead

5-mm coral bead

Adjustable chain closure

Bead tip

Crimp bead

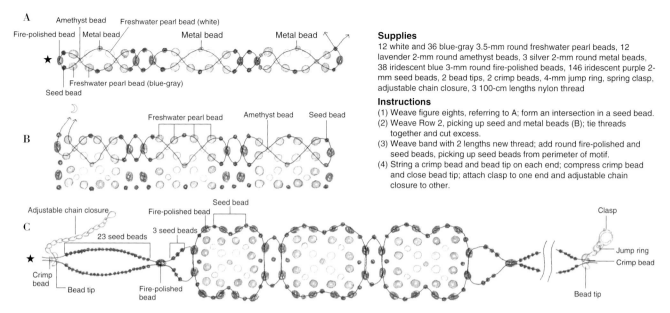

A

Fire-polished bead
Amethyst bead
Metal bead
Freshwater pearl bead (white)
Metal bead
Metal bead
Seed bead
Freshwater pearl bead (blue-gray)

B

Freshwater pearl bead
Amethyst bead
Seed bead

Supplies

12 white and 36 blue-gray 3.5-mm round freshwater pearl beads, 12 lavender 2-mm round amethyst beads, 3 silver 2-mm round metal beads, 38 iridescent blue 3-mm round fire-polished beads, 146 iridescent purple 2-mm seed beads, 2 bead tips, 2 crimp beads, 4-mm jump ring, spring clasp, adjustable chain closure, 3 100-cm lengths nylon thread

Instructions

(1) Weave figure eights, referring to A; form an intersection in a seed bead.
(2) Weave Row 2, picking up seed and metal beads (B); tie threads together and cut excess.
(3) Weave band with 2 lengths new thread; add round fire-polished and seed beads, picking up seed beads from perimeter of motif.
(4) String a crimp bead and bead tip on each end; compress crimp bead and close bead tip; attach clasp to one end and adjustable chain closure to other.

C

Adjustable chain closure
Fire-polished bead
Seed bead
Clasp
23 seed beads
3 seed beads
Jump ring
Crimp bead
Crimp bead
Bead tip
Fire-polished bead
Bead tip

BRACELET 2
BRACELET WITH SQUARE MOTIFS

Mosaic tile was the inspiration for this bracelet. By pulling the nylon thread on the perimeter of each motif, we formed a modified pyramid "B" a marvelous effect!

BRACELET 3
RHINESTONE AND PEARL BRACELET

The cool opulence of this piece comes from the blue notes in the pearl and apatite beads, combined with the sparkle of the rhinestones.

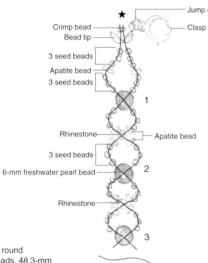

Jump ring

Clasp

Crimp bead
Bead tip

3 seed beads
Apatite bead
3 seed beads

1

Rhinestone — Apatite bead

3 seed beads

6-mm freshwater pearl bead

2

Rhinestone

3

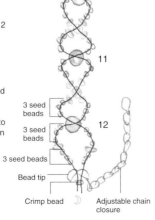

10

11

3 seed beads

3 seed beads

12

3 seed beads

Bead tip

Crimp bead

Adjustable chain closure

Supplies
12 blue-gray 6-mm round freshwater pearl beads, 48 3-mm button apatite beads, 11 aurora 3.5-mm rhinestones in 4-pronged mountings, 156 blue 1-mm seed beads, 2 bead tips, 2 crimp beads, 4-mm jump ring, spring clasp, adjustable chain closure, 2 40-cm lengths nylon thread

Instructions
(1) Weave beads on 2 lengths nylon thread, referring to drawings.
(2) String a crimp bead and bead tip on each end, then compress crimp bead and close bead tip; attach clasp to one end and adjustable chain closure to other.

68

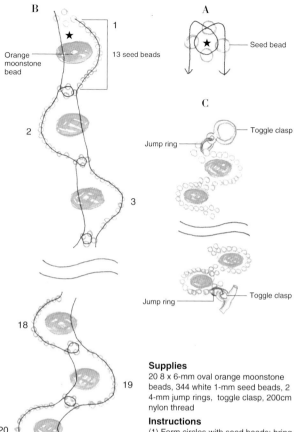

B

Orange moonstone bead

1

13 seed beads

2

3

18

19

20

A

★ —— Seed bead

C

Jump ring

Toggle clasp

Jump ring

Toggle clasp

Supplies
20 8 x 6-mm oval orange moonstone beads, 344 white 1-mm seed beads, 2 4-mm jump rings, toggle clasp, 200cm nylon thread

Instructions
(1) Form circles with seed beads; bring thread out at location shown in A.
(2) Add beads, referring to B; tie threads together and cut excess.
(3) Insert a jump ring into the 4-seed-bead circle at each end of bracelet, then attach clasp.

BRACELET 4
ORANGE MOONSTONE BRACELET

This cheerful bracelet, with its apricot-colored orange moonstone beads surrounded by white seed beads, is sure to put you in a good mood.

69

NECKLACE 1
CARNELIAN NECKLACE

A tumbled carnelian bead is the centerpiece of this magnificent necklace, also decorated with gemstones and gray pearls. The silver beads are the icing on the cake.

Supplies

20-mm tumbled carnelian bead, 56 3-mm labradorite beads, 14 4-6-mm smoky quartz chip beads, 12 gray 8 x 7-mm freshwater pearl rice beads, 25 silver 4-mm bicone crystal beads, 26 4-mm round silver beads, 2 crimp beads, spring clasp, adjustable chain closure, 60cm nylon-coated wire, 20cm wire

Instructions

(1) Make carnelian bead component.
(2) Insert wire into loop above carnelian bead component.
(3) String beads, referring to drawings; add a crimp bead to each end of necklace, then clasp and adjustable chain closure.

Carnelian bead component

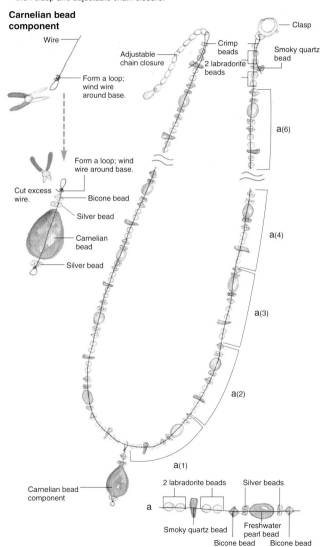

Wire

Form a loop; wind wire around base.

Form a loop; wind wire around base.

Cut excess wire.

Bicone bead

Silver bead

Carnelian bead

Silver bead

Clasp

Crimp beads

Adjustable chain closure

2 labradorite beads

Smoky quartz bead

a(6)

a(4)

a(3)

a(2)

a(1)

Carnelian bead component

a

2 labradorite beads

Silver beads

Smoky quartz bead

Freshwater pearl bead

Bicone bead

Bicone bead

NECKLACE 2
GOTHIC-STYLE NECKLACE

The stark contrast between black and white gives this necklace a Gothic feel. We kept the rest of the necklace simple, since the motif is bold and large.

Supplies

36 white and 48 black 3-mm round fire-polished beads, 4 white and 22 black 4-mm round fire-polished beads, 4 5-mm round fire-polished beads, white 6-mm round fire-polished bead, 4 black 10 x 7-mm designer teardrop beads, 706 black 1.8-mm 3-cut beads, 2 crimp beads, spring clasp, adjustable chain closure, 2 80-cm lengths nylon-coated wire, nylon thread (1 30-cm length, 4 50-cm lengths)

Instructions

(1) Make the flower, referring to A; set one end of thread aside.
(2) Weave with other end of thread, picking up beads from perimeter (B).
(3) Work one round, picking up black fire-polished beads; tie thread to end previously set aside (C).
(4) Repeat Steps (1) to (3) to make 4 motifs; join as shown in D; set one end of thread aside.
(5) String a 6-mm fire-polished bead on other end of thread (E); tie thread to end previously set aside.
(6) Pass nylon-coated wire through a fire-polished bead in motif; center motif on wire; add beads, referring to F.
(7) Align the two strands on each side; attach clasp to one end and adjustable chain closure to other with crimp beads.

Make motifs.

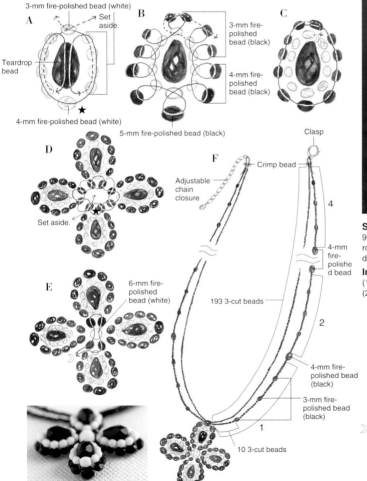

A
3-mm fire-polished bead (white)
Set aside.
Teardrop bead
4-mm fire-polished bead (white)

B
3-mm fire-polished bead (black)
4-mm fire-polished bead (black)
5-mm fire-polished bead (black)

C

D
Set aside.

E
6-mm fire-polished bead (white)

F
Clasp
Crimp bead
Adjustable chain closure
4-mm fire-polished bead
193 3-cut beads
4
2
4-mm fire-polished bead (black)
3-mm fire-polished bead (black)
1
10 3-cut beads

MATCHING RING

We used one of the motifs from the Gothic-style necklace to make this stunning ring. Make a bold fashion statement by wearing these pieces together.

Supplies

9 white and 28 black 3-mm round fire-polished beads, 1 white and 4 black 4-mm round fire-polished beads, black 5-mm round fire-polished bead, black 10 x 7-mm designer teardrop bead, 10 black 2-mm seed beads, 2 50-cm lengths nylon thread

Instructions

(1) Make motive, referring to (1) - (3) of instructions for necklace.
(2) Weave figure eights, referring to drawing; tie threads together, hide in beads and cut excess.

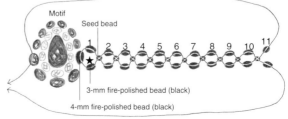

Motif
Seed bead
1 2 3 4 5 6 7 8 9 10 11
3-mm fire-polished bead (black)
4-mm fire-polished bead (black)

73

Supplies

24 5-mm square fluorite beads, 12 purple 7-mm round freshwater pearl beads, 40 green 3-mm bicone crystal beads, 10-mm metal butterfly connector, 2 bead tips, 2 crimp beads, 4-mm jump ring, spring clasp, adjustable chain closure, purple silk thread (2 30-cm lengths, 1 70-cm length and 1 200-cm length), quick-drying glue

Instructions

(1) Allow quick-drying glue to penetrate the end of a 70-cm length silk thread; when glue has partly set, twist end quickly to compress it.

(2) String butterfly connector on center of silk thread; secure connector with a tight knot.

(3) Add a bicone bead, then make a loop; insert the point of a needle into loop and move till loop is immediately above bicone bead; pull thread tightly to form a knot, then remove needle (C).

(4) String more beads, making a knot after each addition; string a crimp bead and a bead tip on each end, then attach clasp to one end and adjustable chain closure to other (D).

(5) Make a tassel from silk thread (E); tie tassel to bottom of butterfly connector.

NECKLACE 3
ASIAN-INSPIRED BUTTERFLY NECKLACE

The silk tassel and metal butterfly connector emphasize the Asian tone of this piece. The purple pearl beads are a nod to the European tradition.

A

Quick-drying glue

Silk thread

B

Tie threads tightly.

Butterfly connector

C

Pull thread.

Slide needle toward bead.

Bicone bead

D

Adjustable chain closure

Crimp bead

Clasp

Bead tip

Jump ring

a(6)

a(3)

a(2)

2 bicone beads

a(1)

Knot

a

Fluorite beads

Bicone beads

Knot

Freshwater pearl bead

Make tassel.

E

Tie 30cm silk thread tightly around tassel.

Cut excess thread.

Remove tassel from cardboard; wind 30cm silk thread around tassel 5mm from top; tie tightly.

Cardboard

4cm

Cut thread here.

Wind 200cm silk thread around cardboard 20 times; cut excess.

Supplies

18 crystal and 22 milky white 3-mm bicone crystal beads, 12 crystal and 44 milky white 4-mm bicone crystal beads, 8 crystal 6-mm bicone crystal beads, 6 crystal aurora 6-mm bicone crystal beads with top holes, 14 crystal aurora 5 x 3-mm spacer beads, 232 silver 2-mm seed beads, 2 crimp beads, spring clasp, adjustable chain closure, 80cm nylon-coated wire, 80cm nylon thread

Instructions

(1) Tape one end of nylon thread to work surface; make a ring of 12 seed beads (A).
(2) String more beads, referring to B.
(3) String milky white bicone beads, picking up seed beads on perimeter (C).
(4) Work around perimeter of snowflake, picking up 3-mm bicone beads (D); bring thread out near other end, remove tape and tie ends together.
(5) String beads on nylon-coated wire (E). Attach a crimp bead to each end of necklace, then clasp to one end and adjustable chain closure to other.

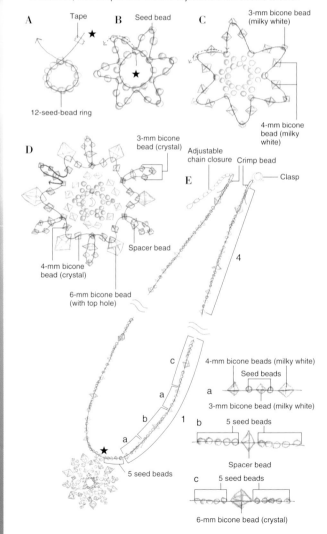

A — Tape
12-seed-bead ring

B — Seed bead

C — 3-mm bicone bead (milky white)
4-mm bicone bead (milky white)

D — 3-mm bicone bead (crystal)
Spacer bead
4-mm bicone bead (crystal)
6-mm bicone bead (with top hole)
5 seed beads

E — Adjustable chain closure
Crimp bead
Clasp
4

c
a
b
a
1

a — 4-mm bicone beads (milky white)
Seed beads
3-mm bicone bead (milky white)

b — 5 seed beads
Spacer bead

c — 5 seed beads
6-mm bicone bead (crystal)

NECKLACE 4
SNOWFLAKE NECKLACE

Milky white and silver beads emphasize the transparent qualities of the brilliant crystal snowflake at the center of this necklace.

Supplies

48 3-mm round green aventurine beads, 8 pink 5-mm round freshwater pearl beads, 6 8-mm round cherry quartz glass beads, 13-mm teardrop cherry quartz glass bead, 12 light pink and 16 pink 3-mm bicone crystal beads, 2 bead tips, 2 crimp beads, 4-mm jump ring, spring clasp, adjustable chain closure, 80cm beige silk thread

Instructions

(1) String beads, alternating them with knots (see p. 74).

(2) Attach a bead tip and crimp bead to each end of necklace, then clasp and adjustable chain closure.

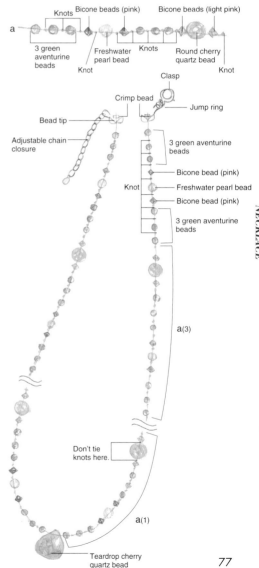

NECKLACE 5
CHERRY PINK NECKLACE

The pale but vibrant cherry pink and green beads in this lovely necklace are punctuated by knots fashioned from beige silk thread.

77

Components

a (Make 5.)

- Jump ring
- Freshwater pearl bead
- Jump ring
- 2-cm eyepin

b (Make 1.)

- Jump ring
- Mother-of-pearl bead
- Jump ring
- 2-cm eyepin

c (Make 1.)

- 3-cm eyepin
- Mother-of-pearl bead

d (Make 1.)

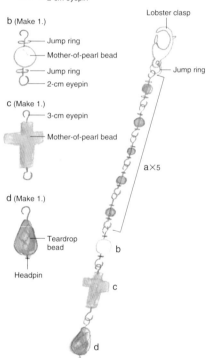

- Teardrop bead
- Headpin

Lobster clasp

Jump ring

a×5

b

c

d

Supplies

5 brown 4-mm round freshwater pearl beads, 6-mm white mother-of-pearl bead, brown 18-mm mother-of-pearl cross, brown 10 x 7-mm designer teardrop bead, 6 2-cm thin eyepins, 3-cm thin eyepin, 2-cm thin headpin, 13 3-cm jump rings, lobster clasp

Instructions

(1) Make Components a-d.
(2) Assemble components, referring to drawings.

CELL PHONE STRAP 1
MOTHER-OF-PEARL CROSS STRAP

A pearl bead and a teardrop bead add interest to the mother-of-pearl cross, as do the eyepins and jump rings that connect the beads.

Supplies

Crystal aurora 15 x 11.5-mm designer teardrop bead, crystal aurora 10 x 7-mm designer teardrop bead, 69 silver 2-mm seed beads, bead tip, crimp bead, 4-mm jump ring, strap finding, 100cm nylon thread

Instructions

(1) String large teardrop bead on center of nylon thread; add seed beads, referring to A.
(2) Add more seed beads (B).
(3) Add small teardrop bead and seed beads (C).
(4) String a bead tip and a crimp bead on end of strap; attach strap finding (D).

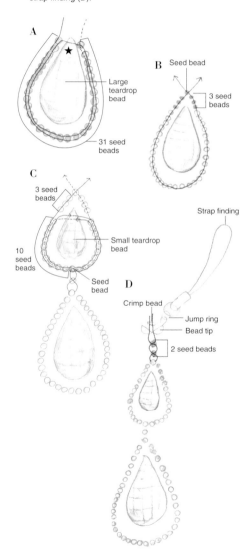

A

★

Large teardrop bead

31 seed beads

B

Seed bead

3 seed beads

C

3 seed beads

10 seed beads

Small teardrop bead

Seed bead

D

Crimp bead

Strap finding

Jump ring

Bead tip

2 seed beads

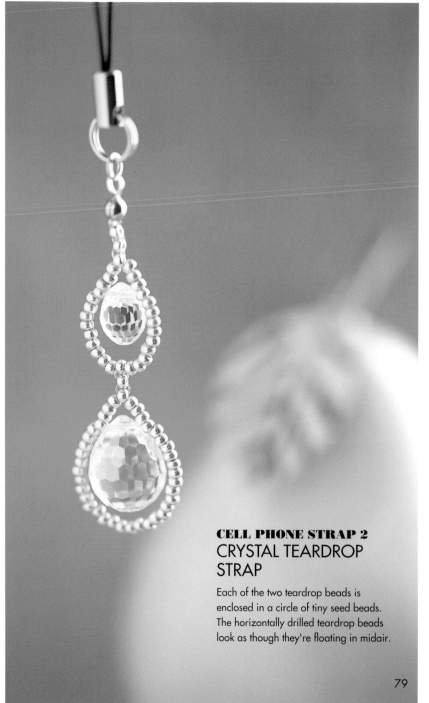

CELL PHONE STRAP 2
CRYSTAL TEARDROP STRAP

Each of the two teardrop beads is enclosed in a circle of tiny seed beads. The horizontally drilled teardrop beads look as though they're floating in midair.

BROOCH
FLOWER BROOCH

The marriage of petals (designer beads of different shapes) and the tiny three-cut beads that frame them add up to a very special brooch. Stabilize the brooch by sewing the motif to a circle of felt so that you can wear it for a long, long time.

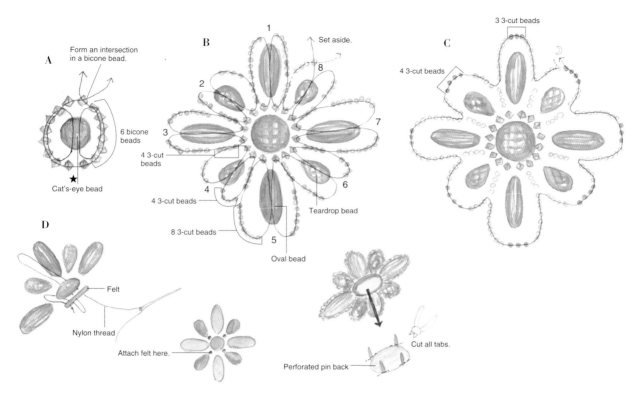

A

Form an intersection in a bicone bead.

6 bicone beads

Cat's-eye bead

B

1

Set aside.

8

2

7

3

4 3-cut beads

4

4 3-cut beads

8 3-cut beads

5

Oval bead

6

Teardrop bead

C

3 3-cut beads

4 3-cut beads

D

Felt

Nylon thread

Attach felt here.

Cut all tabs.

Perforated pin back

Supplies
16 bronze 3-mm bicone crystal beads, 4 black 10 x 7-mm designer teardrop beads, 4 brown 16 x 8-mm designer oval beads, 10-mm brown cat's-eye bead, 156 green 1.8-mm 3-cut beads, 15-mm (diameter) circle of felt, 15-mm (diameter) perforated pin back, nylon thread (1 30-cm length, 1 100-cm length), glue

Instructions
(1) Weave center of flower, referring to A.
(2) Make petals, referring to B; after working one round, set one end of thread aside.
(3) String 3-cut beads on other end of thread, picking up 3-cut beads on perimeter; tie thread to end previously set aside (C).
(4) Sew flower to felt circle with nylon thread; glue piece to pin back (D).

81

BASIC TECHNIQUES

In this section we introduce the basic techniques used in making bead jewelry. Though they may at first seem a bit complex, mastering them will make your work easier and more enjoyable. You can make almost any type of jewelry with just these techniques, among which are weaving and finishing methods, and the use of findings.

WEAVING WITH NYLON THREAD The most basic weaving stitch is the figure eight, which involves stringing beads and forming intersections in beads to create a figure eight. As with the flower and layering stitches, you can create new stitches by changing the point of intersection or the number of beads.

FIGURE EIGHT STITCH: FIRST ROW

(1) String 3 beads on center of nylon thread. The yellow bead is at the center, and the green beads are on either side of it.

(2) String a new (yellow) bead and form a left-right intersection by passing the other end of the nylon thread through the same bead. Thread should extend from both sides of the new bead.

(3) String a green bead on each end of thread.

(4) Form another intersection in a new (yellow) bead.

(5) Pull on both ends of thread. Repeat these steps until you've made the desired number of patterns.

FIGURE EIGHT STITCH: SECOND ROW

(1) At end of first row, form an intersection in a bead in the direction in which you will be working (upward).

(2) String the beads for the second row (3 red beads).

(3) Form an intersection in a bead facing the direction in which you will be working (left).

(4) Pick up purple beads from first row.

(5) String 2 red beads on second row, form an intersection and continue, as before.

FLOWER STITCH

(1) String 7 blue beads on center of nylon thread. Pass both ends of thread through purple bead at the same time.

(2) Pass each end of thread back through 3 blue beads, as shown in photograph.

(3) Pull thread; the purple bead forms the center of the flower, and the blue beads, the petals.

(4) String new blue beads, then form an intersection in a blue bead.

(5) Pull thread.

LAYERED STITCH

(1) Weave foundation row.

(2) String the beads that will form the next layer (2 seed beads and a bicone bead) on both ends of nylon thread. Form an intersection in bicone bead.

(3) String 2 seed beads on each end. Bring thread back to adjoining designer bead on right side and form an intersection.

(4) Pull thread. Continue weaving in the same way.

FINISHING TECHNIQUES

This is the most common finishing technique used with nylon thread. Apply glue to knots to secure them.

Technique used to finish pieces made with nylon thread

(1) Tie ends of thread together.

(2) Tie them again 1-2 times.

(3) Pass one end of thread through an adjoining bead.

(4) Pull the thread, and the knot will disappear inside a bead. Cut excess thread at the edge of a bead.

Working with crimp beads

Crimp beads are a good way to finish necklaces or bracelets without tying knots. They are often used in tandem with bead tips.

Attaching a crimp bead

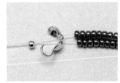   

(1) String a bead tip, then a crimp bead on the end of a length of nylon thread.

(2) Holding the thread taut, compress the crimp bead with flat-nose pliers.

(3) Cut thread, leaving 1-2mm above crimp bead.

(4) Close the bead tip with flat-nose pliers. It's a good idea to leave a 1-mm space between the bead tip and the beads.

Attaching a spring clasp

(1) String a crimp bead, then clasp on the end of a length of nylon-coated wire.

(2) Run wire back through crimp bead and 2 more beads, forming a circle.

(3) Pull wire.

(4) Compress crimp bead with flat-nose pliers.

(5) Cut excess wire with wire-cutters. Follow this same procedure when attaching an adjustable chain closure.

Opening and closing jump rings

Jump rings are used when attaching clasps, or when joining components of a necklace or other piece of jewelry. They must be closed tightly.

(1) Grasp left and right ends of jump ring with pliers. Open jump ring, moving one end up and the other down.

(2) Reverse Step (1) to close.

Opening chain links

(1) Place chain on work surface, and insert the point of an awl into the first link.

(2) Push firmly with the awl to open link.

Attaching beads to perforated findings

Perforated findings are ideal as bases and stabilizers for larger brooches, earrings and necklaces. Components are attached by inserting thread or wire into the holes in the finding.

(1) To keep tabs on finding from damaging beads or nylon thread, use wire-cutters to cut them in half.

(2) Bend tabs down with flat-nose pliers, beginning with 2 adjoining tabs.

(3) Slide top of finding, to which beads have been attached, under bent tabs.

(4) Bend down 2 remaining tabs. Insert tissue paper to avoid damage.

(5) Completed piece

Working with headpins and eyepins

These findings enable you to create and assemble jewelry components. Eyepins are often substituted for chain. The same technique is used to round the ends of both headpins and eyepins.

Rounding the end of a headpin

(1) Insert headpin into a bead. Cut shaft with wire-cutters, leaving a 7 to 8-mm end.

(2) Bend end of headpin, forming a right angle.

(3) Begin rounding end with round-nose pliers.

(4) Stop when shaft is completely rounded, and circle is completely closed.

These headpins have been rounded incorrectly. The one at left was bent too much, the one in the middle was not bent enough, and the one on the right is misaligned.

Joining eyepins

(1) Open rounded end of eyepin with flat-nose pliers, keeping end on a horizontal plane.

(2) Attach component to be joined.

(3) Close end of eyepin with round-nose pliers.

(4) This is how the join should look.

TOOLS AND AUXILIARY MATERIALS

Headpin (top); eyepin (bottom)

Sizes (diameter): thin (0.5mm), standard (0.6mm), thick (0.7mm)

Cord tips (used to secure faux leather cord)

Ear wires

Jump rings

Medium: 4mm
Large: 6mm
Small 3-3.5mm

Adjustable chain closure (bottom)

Spring clasp (top)

Hoop earring finding

Strap finding

Toggle clasp

Lobster clasp

Perforated pin back

Crimp beads (we use the medium size: 2mm)

Bead tip

Mesh tubing (see p. 61)

Pliers

Flat-nose pliers: These have many uses, some of which are opening jump rings and compressing crimp beads.

Round-nose pliers: Used for rounding the ends of headpins and eyepins.

Wire-cutters: Used to cut headpins, eyepins and wire.

Stringing materials

Thin nylon thread

Nylon-coated wire (we use 0.24-0.36mm wire for the projects in this book) Jewelry made with nylon-coated wire is finished with crimp beads or bead tips, since the wire cannot be tied.

Wire (We use 0.4mm wire for the projects in this book. Wire can be used to join components in place of headpins or eyepins.)

Silk thread
Silk thread adds a luxurious feel to a piece of jewelry. It is used to make necklaces and tassels.

Miscellaneous supplies

Ring stick
Ring sticks are used by jewelers to size rings. They can also be used to bend eyepins.

Jeweler's awl
This is used to open chain links.

Beading trays
The larger tray is lined with fabric to keep beads from rolling around. It is easy to extract beads from the small triangular tray.

Glue
We apply glue to knots in nylon thread and to compressed crimp beads to secure them. We recommend two-part epoxy.